Jolly Survives
FROM THE FAILED BEAN

Jolly Survives
From The Failed Bean

Prabhat Ranjan Bhattacharyya

Translated by Abhirup Bhattacharyya

Chitrangi

Published by Chitrangi, A-10/1, Amarabati,
Sodepur, Calcutta 700110 INDIA
Contact: chitrangifoundation@gmail.com

First edition (Paperback): September, 2017
Front cover photograph: Plabon Das
Cover design: *Chitrangi*
ISBN 9789385782442

Price: INR 250 / USD 10.00

Department of Nephrology
Christian Medical College
Vellore (India)

Translator's Note

I never thought in the wildest of my dreams to write a book on and that too a translation of my father's work. At times, in life you get things which you least expect and that gives an unparalleled satisfaction. Translation of *Kidney Ruddho Jibon Yuddho* begun almost three months ago, and now that it is ready for publication I feel extremely contented, that I took up the challenge, although I tried by all means to defer Baba's wish. It had just been a year since the Bengali book was released, and I was not sure whether the English version would be well received. The other reason was more personal — I did not want to awaken the demons from the past, for I remain wary of my emotions even now; I was never confident of impersonalizing myself while writing which Baba did exquisitely in his book. I believe the original book reflected on the storm and struggle that larked over my parents' lives and it's a mammoth responsibility to translate the text for a bigger audience. I've been witnessing all events since I was eight-year old; I've assimilated their whole journey within my being. In these three months that I spent in translating the original book, it has become a habit of re-living those moments, as a montage of images and happenings taken straight out of the past and played in front of me.

Poet, novelist and literary translator, Boris Pasternak, once said—

> "Literature is the art of discovering something extraordinary about ordinary people, and saying with ordinary words something extraordinary."

This book will not only let people compose themselves and decide on the course of action, but it also infuses in their positivity, mental grit, faith and ultimately the only thing we live with, i.e. hope!

While I was in Pondicherry University, we had a paper titled "Translation: Theory and Practice" and I never knew I would actually have to keep getting back to those classes and lectures to understand what it meant to go for a "sense-for-sense" translation and/or "word-for-word." While translating Baba's book, *Kidney Ruddho Jibon Yuddho,* I understood that I would have to stick to the basic layers of the original text, and going by the original author's nature would have to move between both "sense-for-sense" and "word-for-word." The greatest challenge that a translator faces is to replicate the emotions presented in the translated text as faithful to the source text, maintaining the idea and perception of the source author. I was faced with the problem of using certain words from Bengali which if translated into English would lose its sweetness and relevance, and thus, prompting me to keep them as-it-is in the original. Language barriers will always remain and therefore certain "culture-specific" terms have been left as-it-is, for the readers to enjoy the authenticity.

Each and every language has its nuances and limitations; therefore a translator has to work within all these parameters, but all the while keeping in mind that the book must be an interesting read. The ulterior motive of this book is to reach out to the national and international readers about kidney failure and transplant, where in the book can be of help to families with time.

Abhirup Bhattacharyya
12th August, 2017
Calcutta, India

Author's Note

I prefer reading books which have lucid language and always favour presenting intricate situations in the easiest manner, avoiding any complications. Colloquially and while writing, I generally take the easy-peasy route. My motive was to maintain this narrative style in my Bengali book whereof my readers could easily connect to our journey.

When my son, Abhirup, finally decided to take the plunge into translating my book, I specified to him that the facile style of the Bengali book must be maintained; not an ounce of artificiality and exaggeration can find its place in the translation. I further mentioned that in the English book, he must consult me while referring to the treatment-related phrases. I believe by his own style, Abhirup has duly succeeded in his tryst. This is his first endeavor and I sincerely hope you all shower your blessings on him, wishing him luck in the future.

For my Bengali book *Kidney Ruddho Jibon Yuddho* and Abhirup's translation *Jolly Survives: From the Failed Bean* I would primarily thank my long-standing friend, Dr. Kiriti Sengupta. It was he who had first soaked the seeds of this book in my head, last year, and I'm not just indebted to him for being the publisher of the books. If he had not taken the initiative, most probably the Bengali book would never have been written. Right from the printing, publishing of the book and later on all the necessary steps to make the book reach the readers, he and his companion Mr. Bitan Chakraborty's contribution is unparalleled. Currently, their contribution behind the English book, and Dr. Sengupta's idea behind the title of the translated book is commendable.

Before concluding, I would like to thank the doctors and nurses of the Nephrology department, Christian Medical College, Vellore and various other patients with whom I interacted, for encouraging us to translate the Bengali book into English. Last but not the least, around whom the book is revolving, Jolly, whose unparalleled assistance propelled me and my son to give vent to our feelings.

Prabhat Ranjan Bhattacharyya
Calcutta, India

CONFESSIONS

The words expressed here in this book, is actually a partial re-telling of my life- of the struggles that has been encountered by my family. Since the inception of the idea for this book, I have tried to be as authentic as possible, not having exaggerated a wee bit for the sake of attracting the attention of the readers. This books is all about how my wife, Jolly fought against the odds of Chronic Renal Failure (CRF), and how she, my son Abhirup and myself left no stones unturned to make out a happy and prosperous life. Having spent more than 25 years of my life with Jolly, it comes with no doubt that her problems were mine, and vice versa. Throughout my endeavor it has been really difficult to keep aside my emotions and turn their waves into words. I really believe that all of you will be able to relate in some way or the other to the incidents mentioned here. It is a true life story that revolves around three souls, heavily dependent on each other, and by the end of the book, you shall see how 'jolly' we have remained, in-spite of all the challenges thrown against us by Him.

I'm well aware of all my limitations and weaknesses, and therefore I do not build castles in the air. I aspired to be a footballer when I was a kid, but that had to be immersed into the Holy Ganges at the age of 19, having come face-to-face with the harsh realities of life. Thereafter fighting against all odds, facing all ups-and-downs of life, I have gradually tried to turn the immature 'me' into a mature and complete one. There has always been the endeavor to believe that if I ever face any difficult situation, I shall not bow down. You can say, that I believe if we are honest in our journey and have a positive mindset, then we have enough ammunition to fight against anything and everything. I have always tried to teach my son one ultimate philosophy — "Life is not always about winning or losing, but about how you fight, about all the grit and determination and the mindset."

THE BEGINNING

I have been hit by the Cupid number of times in my life, and that has all been at a very young age; and even in that, the journey has not been smooth. When I thought of giving all my heart and soul into one such affair, it took a lot of time for me to realize that it was not my cup-of-tea, and by the time I could detach myself I was mentally very disturbed. To bring myself out of those tatters, I deliberately engaged myself into various avenues. I had almost made myself believe that 'love' was never to happen to me, and more so, never would a marriage or a family!

I was barely managing myself, staying at a rented flat in Baguiati, in North Kolkata, working as a Medical Representative, for a company with its head office in Mumbai; when it suddenly packed its bags and left. I waited for four months at my native place, Purbasthali, a village in the Burdwan district of West Bengal, after which I joined a new company and fortunately, they posted me at Burdwan, which is a District town a few hours from my native place. Purbasthali is a village of rich heritage on the banks of Bhagirathi, around 8 kilometers from the holy land of Shri Chaitanya

Mahaprabhu, Nabadwip. Purbasthali has been historically, culturally, spiritually and educationally very rich.

Coming back to my work life during this period, I started working in and around Burdwan, where I stayed at the 'All West Bengal Sales Representatives' Union' rest house, and again approximately 10 days at my native residence. Along with the job and its intricacies, I continued my passion in the field of cultural activities like drama, recitation etcetera, along with physical exercise and various other activities.

Around this time, an acquaintance of mine took me along with him to a house, which on entering seemed to be much more modern than the contemporary structures that I had seen in and around Purbasthali. I got acquainted with the owner of the house and his wife. I must tell you here a little bit about the person with whom I accompanied because he had played a huge role in striking off a tie with this house. The acquaintance who took me to this house was Mr. Shyamal Kumar Pathak, who was actually a school teacher and also known as an electronic mechanic in the locality, whom I used to dearly call Dada. He had come to this house on account of the owner's interest to change the old 'valve-state' television to a modern 'solid-state' one, and therefore we took the television set, only to return it after a few days. Coincidentally, on the day of returning the set I was there, and I got to know the family better. I came to know the owner of the house was an Ex-serviceman at the Indian Navy, and after his early retirement they had shifted and constructed this house. They had two daughters, out of which the elder had a vocation in Kolkata; the younger one attended the Nabadwip College, and a very young son who used to study at a primary school in Purbasthali. One thing that struck me hard during many such early visits was that the two sisters would converse mainly in English and Hindi, which to be very frank I did not like. Thereafter I did not get any opportunity to visit their house or meet them. Suddenly one fine day, I met the two sisters at a doctors' chamber at Nabadwip, where I had gone in lieu of my job. We three returned together and on the way back I got the opportunity to know them well and about their lives. I came to know that due to the nature of their dads' work, they had spent certain span of time in the cities of Goa, Mumbai, Kochin (Kochi), Delhi and few others. They opened their hearts and spoke how they could not get along with the contemporary circumstances and found it difficult to spend their time. Although the younger sister had made a circle of her own due to her college-life, the elder one had left her job because she could not bear the hassles of daily en-routes to and fro between Purbasthali and Kolkata. Therefore I don't think I need to explain the forlorn condition this young lady had to go through, staying behind at home with no friend or company. At this juncture I pitched in an idea to her saying, "You two can visit my house, where you might find good company in my two sisters, and thereby be much more at ease." One of the main reason as to why I had given them the invitation to my house was that me and my siblings were all pretty eloquent in Hindi, since our father had been in the Railways, and we had spent an ample amount of time at Katihar, which is a small town in North Bihar. I also believed that staying in touch with my sisters the two ladies would be able to even out the rough edges of their Bengali language.

Very soon their whole family visited our house on the occasion of *Bijoya Dashami* Thereafter the elder sister would often visit our house, spend time with my sisters talking and playing badminton, and by dusk return to her house. On the days that would get a bit late my father would escort her till her house, and that duty would come upon me on the weekends. Their house was about 7-8 minutes walking distance from ours, and on the way back we would talk of nothing very paramount. What is to be noted here is that I was then standing at the footsteps of 30, and it would be fanciful that the Cupid could strike me then! More so, she was not that beautiful to attract a 'to-be-30' man who had tasted various experiences and by then had believed that love was not his cup-of-tea! However there was something enigmatic about this lady- her behavior, her jolly ways of making everyone feel at ease, having no airs of pride about her and the all-encompassing alacrity in all ways; but I did not want to express my weakness to her. Soon, it was time for the very famous *Kartik Puja* festival (*Kartik-Puja* is a Hindu or Jain holy festival celebrated in the month of November, and in Purbasthali it is celebrated imitating the *Ras Yatra* of Nabadwip) of Purbasthali, and the two sisters along with my siblings spent their time gleefully. There was a child-like innocence in her eyes and expressions which gave me a lot of satisfaction. Few days later when she visited our house, my mood was not at its best, and seeing me morose, she inquired, to which I replied nothing. I took off with her to her house, and on the way back told her somewhat of the problem. The patient listener consoled me. I felt relieved. I was glad that I had her by me.

On the next day I left for Burdwan, and this was the first time that I felt a vacuum- I missed her presence. The simplicity of her was an enigma and I kept getting reminded of her. I knew I would not be able to meet her that weekend since she would be attending a marriage ceremony of one of her cousin, away from Purbasthali. I was already under a lot of pressure due to 'sales-closing', and not being able to meet her for such a long period made me utterly restless. I made up my mind to disclose my strong feelings to her the next time, and since the English New Year was approaching I bought a pen and a greetings card in English which had words apt, subtly to express my feelings. I returned to my native residence on the eve of New Year, and not being able to restrain myself, went to their house to meet her. She said she would visit our place the next morning, which was the first day of a new year, and more so a Sunday!

On the first day of January she visited our house, wished everyone on English New Year, and then came to me. I did not waste much time before giving her the pen and the greetings card, where I had added two more lines to express that she had occupied a vast space of my heart and mind. What transpired soon after did not give me solace; she took the pen, read the card with a twinkle in her eyes, and returned the card saying, "I cannot take this with me. Keep it with you." The succeeding day I was supposed to leave for Burdwan, but in hope to know her reply to my proposal, I deterred my leave. In the evening when she came, something made me feel that the letter had not missed its mark;

The next week I directly confronted her about my proposal. She told me that if her parents had nothing to refuse, she did not have any problem, but she asked me about my profession, income, my aspirations, about what I like or want from my life, and so on. She was open enough to express her wish to work in the future and the profession that she had chosen was only to be found in and around Kolkata. Here I must tell you that she had completed her diploma in Secretarial Practice from Young Women's Christian Association (Y.W.C.A), Delhi. She had had an experience working in Delhi and then in Kolkata. Naturally, she wanted to work in Kolkata in the future and settle here. She was quite vocal about what she wanted, and as per my nature I too did not hold back about myself. I very well gauged from her way of enquiring about me and my life, that she was very mature and did not allow emotions to get over her. She was then 22, and it would have been natural for her to be driven by emotions. I was then nearing 3 decades of my life, and naturally instinctive emotions did not drive me; but isn't love very much instinctive?!

As promised I wrote her a letter, telling her everything about my family, its past and present, about my siblings, the relationship that I shared with them, about what I like or my wishes, my profession, my income, me and my family's economic status, my future aspirations, and so on. I even mentioned my expectations from her. I intentionally stuck to Bengali while writing the letter, except for instances where I had to use English; and I made it a point that she writes back in Bengali, as much as possible. I even told her that the portions which were not comprehensible by her, she should mark them out, and on meeting her I would explain it. My only intention was to develop her mother-tongue: and let me tell you, we were very much successful in our pursuit.

The succeeding week I handed her a letter, she read it and the next day I explained to her the portions which were incomprehensible. Soon, I received a reply to my letter, and our love-affair was off to a smooth start by the means of love-letters. We would also meet twice a week for an hour or so. It had also become our habit to let each other know about our daily happenings. Once we had contemplated and decided about our future, I said to her, "I take complete responsibility about my house. I shall take care of that. But you must disclose everything to your parents and if needed I shall be there." From the onset, she had told me that her father was very strict and therefore she could not confide about the relationship to him. She even declined when I suggested that she could tell her mother. Very naturally, I was pretty much afraid to face her father with the proposal of marrying his daughter; but trying to be manful I said, "Fine. I'll go and speak to your parents. Let's hope for the best, and if not, we shall then see what we can do!" I have never had the habit of keeping things at bay and therefore did not waste much time to decide that I would meet them in the next two days.

Let me tell u here that during this time she was learning *Rabindra Sangeet* under Mr.

Dayal Hari Santra (a.k.a Khudiram*da*), and was an integral part of his institution called *Purbasthali Songeet Samaj*. Myself being pretty much interested in cultural events and quite close to Khudiram*da*, I was a usual visitor to his place. I got enough time to interact with her, during *Saraswati Puja* at the above mentioned institution. We decided amongst us, that, on the day of immersion of the Saraswati idol, when her father would not be present, she would also come out and I would meet her mother and disclose to her about our decision. In all probability, that day was 12th February, 1989. I met her mother and told her everything that had transpired, and she said that she never thought this was coming. She even said that she did not have the courage to tell it to her other half and that I myself had to confess my love for his daughter, to him. Therefore, I decided to face some chin music, very next day met her father, and said to him, "I have something to tell you." He replied, "I know Jolly's mother has told me everything." However, after having met her father, I understood that he was not as difficult to face as much I had been told. He told me that he would counsel with his father and elder brother, and have a talk with Jolly. Later on he even advised his daughter to think of all the pros-and-cons and take the step forward.

During those days, the issues of inter-caste marriages were discerned by the society, and that happened more in the rural areas due to their conservativeness. Purbasthali was a stronghold of the Brahmins (highest caste or community among the Hindus), and our family was one of them. Moreover, we are known as a special class of Brahmin, told as *Vaidik* community. Though I never cared about such meaningless caste segregations, but like many mothers, my mother had some inhibitions regarding me marrying Jolly, because she was not from the Brahmin community. Like every mother, she too ideally would have preferred an attractive girl for her son, but Jolly was far from that, in terms of skin-tone and looks that too caused a bit of negative reaction from my mother. I knew that my decision of marrying Jolly was not wrong and therefore nobody could stop me, so I persuaded Ma and kept trying to make her understand. However, my Baba although was very religious, never bothered about meaningless stuffs as caste-division, and thereafter whenever she would visit our house, he was very endearing towards her.

Our relationship sailed smoothly for the next two years. She would visit our house, and I would see off her till her house. The extra incentive now was that I would go to their house, sit for hours and talk to her family members. We would make good use of the freedom at times, going to watch a movie at a nearby hall in Nabadwip, or some cultural program, and even she came twice to meet me in Kolkata, while I had gone there for work. With nobody to notice us, we would roam around the *City of Joy* freely, breathing in the fresh essence of love. During our courtship days, writing letters never ceased, rather it increased. There must be around a 100 letters in total from both the sides! Since I loved poetry and even tried a hand at writing a few lines here and there, I would write verses in lucid *Bangla* for Jolly in the letters. Meanwhile, in the month of October 1989, due to some problems at my workplace, I began looking out for new job opportunities, gave numerous interviews, and eventually on January 1990, got placed in a new company, as Kolkata headquarter. In the previous company where I would get 1500 per month, the new company offered me 2500. Initially I would daily travel to and fro between Purbasthali and Kolkata, which I soon realized would be extremely strenuous over a period of time. Therefore I decided to stay put at my Choto Mashima's house in Kolkata, and return to Purbasthali for the weekend. As days passed by, my father fell ill, and due to lack of good medical facilities, we had to shift him to the Marwari Relief Society, in Kolkata, where he stayed admitted for almost a month. Once he became a little better, we returned to Purbasthali, but Baba was already suffering from a multiple health issues. He had no savings, so with whatever little I earned, the eldest of my two sisters got married to a close friend of mine on 4th August, 1990, based at another close friend's house in Kolkata. My family will forever be grateful to this friend. In the meanwhile preparations began for my marriage, and although everything was on my shoulders, a few elders from my family went to Jolly's house, and decided that 23rd January, 1991 would be the auspicious day.

I was neck deep into economic instability, but we went about with our plan. Jolly's family too chipped in when we needed economic assistance, which I obviously returned in due course of time. Eventually, we got married and everything went off smoothly.

Post-marriage my routine was daily travelling between Purbasthali and Kolkata and when needed would stay at my younger maternal aunt's house in Kankurgachi. On the other hand, Jolly was adjusting into her new environment, managing her new family, and I knew it pretty well that it would be a little difficult for her to come from her family and adjust into mine. I had advised her, "When you are in Purbasthali with my parents, try following the customs shown by my Ma. Try making things around you, your own, even though I know it is difficult." In the same way later on when we shifted to Kolkata, I told Ma to try adjusting to Jolly's ways. We found conducive results in both the cases; although it was instant in Jolly's case, a bit time-consuming for Ma.

Very soon after our marriage we started making plans of shifting to somewhere in or around Kolkata, and Jolly started attending interviews for the post of secretary after constantly following advertisements in the daily *The Statesman*. She applied at nearly twenty places, out of which some four or five called for an interview pretty soon. Things were slowly but steadily falling into place- Jolly landed up with a job, and on the same day we decided on the rented place in Srirampur, a small town in the Hooghly district, suburb of Kolkata. Jolly joined the new job on 23rd April, 1991, and our new life started. We started travelling from Srirampur to Howrah station and to our respective workplaces, and again in the evening returning home. On Saturdays, we would catch the evening train from Howrah station to Purbasthali, and return by the Monday morning mail. It was hectic, but it was something we had planned, and wanted. We were slowly starting to put wings to our hopes and aspirations.

Baba's condition was fast deteriorating in the meanwhile. He had to be shifted to Nil Ratan Sircar Medical College and Hospital (N.R.S), Kolkata, which altered our daily routine again. It did not affect my routine much because NRS Medical College and Hospital was one of the most important working territories of mine. It was very hectic for us every day to make time and visit father at the hospital, keep a regular check on whether he was eating properly, his medicines, give him time and never neglect his needs; far more difficult for Jolly than me. She would daily wake up at 5 in the morning, leave for office around 8, meet me after her work got off at the hospital and return home with me around 11 at night. More so, after returning home she would prepare our dinner and then in the morning our breakfast, and separately food for Baba. Sundays and holidays were nothing different for us, only that we would leave for hospital a bit late. Father's situation was constantly deteriorating, with one by one many complications catching up- malina, enlarged prostate, pleural effusion, anemia, tuberculosis, and at the end chronic renal failure. Doctors later on asked us to take my father back, take good care of him, and regularly keep them updated. We returned to Purbasthali, would stay there for the weekend and return straight to work on Monday. Soon the doctors decided to treat him for tuberculosis, on the basis of my feedback. They also advised to transfuse him two bottles of blood. Soon we arranged it in Purbasthali Primary Health Centre, and these worked magically for him. During the time he was admitted at NRS Medical College and Hospital, he was under Dr. R. K. Dutta Roy, who was very gentle and used to address even his students formally. I was amazed at how he diagnosed my father's ailment, just on the virtue of my feedback.

So you see this way we fought and spent our days, weeks and months after our nuptial. We could not find some time to even watch some movie, honeymoon was a far-fetched dream or hope. I was born may be to fight my whole life, but I always felt bad for Jolly. She was a modern girl, born and brought up far away from the contemporary everyday

Bengali society, and I could not offer her any peace or stability of any sort. However, her mental strength and will was incomparable to anybody I had seen till then. In all such critical stages, she never showed displeasure; rather she was always hands on and mature to handle all situations. Baba was more or less getting better, and out of nowhere my office presented its workers with a week of paid holiday trip to Bangalore and Mysore in November, 1991. It was a necessary break for us. Again in the month of May, 1992 we went for two days to Digha, a seaside town in West Bengal, in the northern end of the Bay of Bengal.

It was extremely challenging to daily travel from Srirampur to Kolkata, stay in a single room rented house and use a single general washroom there. We had no other option and therefore we had to adjust to these challenges. We had the intentions of shifting to a rented house in Kolkata, and that started off very soon. While returning from office, at times we would scout for rented houses and again during the weekends or on holidays. Those who have been through the horrendous experience of running behind 'middlemen' to get hold of rented place, must easily be able to relate to how an arduous experience it might have been! It was an inexplicable episode, such that some would ask whether we were government employees; not just that, whether we were working in the bank! Then, whether anybody practiced music, or whether we had kids and whatever reason the landlords could come up with! However, after a long and laborious pursuit, overcoming such insane inquisitions, we landed up with a two room flat in the month of April, 1993, in Baguiati. After buying the necessary stuffs for our new place, Jolly started making preparations. She single handedly managed everything, and I do not deserve any accolades here. Anything and everything I speak about her ingenuous abilities would be less. I have always been someone who would be happy at just spending days, without having neither high hopes nor dreams; I had let go off my dreams long back. Life was a struggle for me, and I was simply elated when something extra came by my way. It would never occur to me that I should augur my hopes and I had accepted that I needed to find solace from whatever little I could achieve.

Life changing news came upon us as soon as we shifted to our new rented house. Jolly became pregnant and the news shuffled our lives totally, more for her. With time, eventually on 3rd February, 1994, we were blessed with a son. Within a week, we visited Purbasthali, where Jolly stayed for three months, including before and after our son's birth, after which she rejoined her job. When we had returned from Purbasthali this time, my Ma accompanied us. Thereafter, just like any other middle-class family, when we would leave for work, she would look after our son.

Our life was filled with happiness and prosperity. Life took its own course. Monthly twice, I would visit my native place due to job-related necessities and therefore was very much aware of my father's health. I was quite aware that his health was deteriorating, and he was constantly being taken to Nabadwip and down to Kolkata. In the meantime, my younger sister Rupa's marriage was fixed, and this was also due to Jolly's attempts. On 5th February, 1996, Rupa tied the knot from Purbasthali. Our two-year contract of the rented house was getting over and we shifted to a bit spacious two-bedroom flat, as soon as Rupa got married.

It was not much time that we had shifted to the new place when my father's condition worsened and we brought him to Kolkata. We regularly shifted him from hospital to our house and this went on for quite some time. In the meantime his enlarged prostate was operated, and then he was diagnosed with CRF, meaning Chronic Renal Failure. His dialysis began soon. At that time, dialysis was not at all common at any random hospital, and I could not afford the expenses at some private hospital. Therefore, we again kept him under the doctors at NRS Medical College and Hospital. NRS Medical College and Hospital had just then started off with the dialysis unit under the Medicine Department. Apart from that no government hospital except The Institute of Post-Graduate Medical Education and Research (popularly known as PG Hospital) and Seth Sukhlal Karnani Memorial Hospital (S.S.K.M) had the dialysis unit at its disposal.

According to the rules, NRS Medical College and Hospital did not have any arrangements for dialysis for the outdoor-patients. Therefore when the doctors would advise for dialysis, we usually admitted my father and the dialysis unit call for the session as per their convenience. Renal failure related many complications slowly started to surface, and so were daily visitors there. Once, even for a stretch of 8 months my father had to be admitted there, and you can easily fathom the pain he had to go through, in the sunset of his life. What could have gone over our family at that time is very difficult to elucidate in a few words or lines. But as I have always maintained, maybe I was born with the ill-fate to struggle and Jolly who could have had a better life had she not been my wife. It is a pain I can never explain or even try to pronounce in words!

This book is all about Jolly. Here, I am a petty person, but since the time we tied the knot, our lives have become one, and with time our bonding has grown from strength to strength. As the book proceeds you shall get to know why I have continuously maintained that her positive mentality and mental grit has made me look at her in awe. I have never met anybody like her and have learnt a lot from her. Life took examinations one after another, and she just surpassed them all with ease. Her sense of discipline was immaculate. I can never remember seeing her tired or unenthusiastic regarding any work. I have always seen her taking responsibility with a smile. Her never-say-die-attitude has always been inspirational for us. At certain difficult stages, even if I had lost my patience, I can never remember seeing Jolly lose her patience. Being prim-and-proper in anything that she touched was a quality, which she had undoubtedly gained from her genes. Both of us are very open-minded, and therefore there would generally be a lot of clamourings, but we always had full belief and trust on each other, and that was where we sailed through anything thrown against us.

Our new chapter that started on 3rd February, 1994, had grown up fighting his own odds against typhoid, ready to join school. We started looking at our options and side-by-side for our own apartment. We were juggling too many things at the same time- my father and his deteriorating condition, interview at various schools for our son's admission, staying on the lookout of an apartment and with that our jobs. We had named our son Abhirup. We did not have to go through much headache of getting our son admitted to a good school. Although I always wanted my son to study in some mediocre Bengali-Medium school, Jolly always had the eye out for a good English-medium school. Keeping to her wish, Abhirup got admitted to The Frank Anthony Public School, Kolkata, which in the last decade or more has become one of the most sought after schools in the city. We eventually landed up with a two-room flat according to our financial condition. Yet, we were never that well off to pay the whole amount and buy the house. Jolly then suggested that we approach the bank for a housing loan, and I was dead against taking loan. I would never do something that was not within my reach, and taking loan was equivalent to being in debt! I was well aware that majority of the people would take loan from the banks, but I always believed that I would only get a house when I was capable of earning it. Since my childhood I have been very wary of taking loans of any kind, even now I don't prefer it and therefore I do not have a credit card. I was never much convinced with this idea of her, but I had to accede to her way. There was still some time for the flat to get completely ready and be handed over to us, so, that gave us some time to get the things ready. Jolly took the whole responsibility of arranging for the down payment, security deposit and monthly loan repayment where as I would keep running to the bank and behind the promoter. Jolly arranged for some amount by selling off all her jewelries and from her past savings. We paid our promoter, but suffered stumbling blocks while paying the security deposit in the bank. Again, evading and fighting against all odds, we finally got the key to our flat and had our house-warming ceremony on 14th November, 1999.

On the other hand, enlarged prostate issues of Baba resurfaced and our journey to-and-fro between home and hospital resumed. When we entered our new house, Baba was with us, and within 15 days, on 4th December, 1999, he was again hospitalized. This time, proving the doctors wrong and nullifying all their attempts, Baba left for the heavenly abode on 21st January, 2000. On 20th I had left for Purbasthali for my work, and that night itself Jolly called me up urging me to return as soon as possible, seeing my Baba's condition deteriorating. Next day I returned and straightaway went to the hospital. Around 4 in the evening I returned home and in the evening, around 6, Jolly called me up to give the sad news. Baba breathed his last in front of Jolly and my two brothers, Bacchu and Laltu. I did not have the courage to tell the truth to Ma or my six-year old son. Later on, I completed all the last rites in the righteous way.

Here if I do not mention about a few people who stood by me during my Baba's ailment, it will be an unpardonable mistake on my part. I can never forget those workers at the hospital, who would go regularly and visit the ward, talk to the doctors, and when needed would get medicines for Baba. My wife, brothers, some near-and-dear ones were always there, but the relationship that I made with a few workers at the hospital, has remained intact till date. I am a person who can befriend people in a jiffy, and that is what happened with the doctors, workers, security guards, liftman, and whoever I met there. I have always tried maintaining healthy relationship with people, and for that have received spontaneous heartfelt wishes and blessings, which have always given me extra courage to fight my battles in life.

Once Baba left, our house had a big void. It seemed really different without him around. Baba used to love Jolly and Abhirup dearly, so it is quite understandable how they felt without him around. He was a doting father-in-law and a Dadu. Jolly was very much mature to have endured this emptiness in the family, but it is quite understandable how Abhirup must have felt having lost his only partner. However, at that age he showed immense maturity, but it was Ma who suffered the greatest blow. She had never been mentally very strong and that just swelled up with the passing away of her 'almost 50 years' of partner. With age, she had started suffering from high blood pressure, atrial fibrillation and insomnia, which became serious with the passing away of her husband. The new century was waiting to throw up humongous ordeals, of which, we were naturally never prepared!

THE BALL STARTS ROLLING

We were already quite ruffled up with Ma's illness when one morning Jolly woke up to find her fingers and feet all swollen up. I advised her to meet a doctor while returning from office. During her childhood she had been diagnosed with rheumatic fever, and for almost 6 years, up to the age of 15 she had to be under medication. Apart from that, she had eczema on her hands since childhood and her medication for this had been very sporadic; at times homoeopathy, again at times allopathy. If you remember, I had mentioned in the beginning, that one day I had met Jolly and her sister at a doctor's chamber in Nabadwip. She had actually gone there to meet a renowned skin specialist (Dermatologist) who would visit Nabadwip once a month. Thereafter when I would meet her, I could notice her face swelling up, and after checking her prescriptions understood that the doctor had prescribed her oral steroids. I explained to her the ill-effects of steroids, and then, without my notice, she stopped those steroids (which should not be stopped abruptly) and started visiting a local homoeopathy doctor. Thereafter, she developed an affinity to homoeopathy medicine, and whenever something small would crop up, she would visit the nearest homoeopathy doctor. The day she noticed her hands, feet and face swollen, she went to meet the homoeopathy doctor near to our house in Baguiati while returning from office, who gave her a few medicines and asked her to check the levels of Urea and Uric Acid in her blood. Next day, at a nearby laboratory, she gave blood samples for examination and on my insistence, Creatinine and Hemoglobin too. In the evening when we got the report, I could not believe my eyes. Everything was a little over the normal levels. Just to re-check we got check-up done at two more places, and the results at all the three places were more-or-less the same. Creatinine was between 1.5-1.6, Urea 45-50, Hemoglobin 7.5-7.7 and so on. I was left speechless, as if I could not believe a single thing that had transpired. I started fearing the worst, since I had been a medical representative, and again handled Baba for years before he breathed his last. I had been educated over those years that Urea, Creatinine levels had a lot to speak about our kidney functions and therefore I could understand the threat looming large over our head, especially Jolly. I pretty well understood seeing the reports that another intriguing and difficult chapter of my life was about to enfold, but I could not fathom why He was testing a disciplined, hard-working, health-aware and mentally strong person like Jolly in this way. As the proverb by James H Augey goes, "Hope is the last lingering light of the human heart. It shines when every other is put out." With this flickering light of hope in our heart, we started off for the traumatic and daunting fight. We were two souls now with our back against the wall, understanding that the road ahead is not going to be easy.

Since my working territory was at NRS Medical College and Hospital, I first took Jolly there. There was no proper Nephrology department, so we went to the Urology department. After being under check for a few months, the doctors came out with a report that even though there was no change in the size of the two kidneys, there were changes in the Urea-Creatinine levels. So we consulted the then very renowned Nephrologist Dr. Bijan Bhattacharya, in November, 2001, who advised we do an ultrasonography of the kidneys. Proving my fears right, he told me that Jolly had Chronic Renal Failure (CRF), and for further report a biopsy had to be conducted. Having seen Baba in the last years of his sufferings, both of us had understood what it meant. All hell broke loose on us! We knew by then the basics of CRF, which the common people neither then, nor now understand. Pretty much against both of our nature, we did not discuss anything regarding the ailment amongst us. We were shell-shocked at all that had transpired. For a few months neither of us, ever brought up the topic during our interactions, although we discussed everything else happening in our day-to-day lives. I could pretty well understand what was happening inside Jolly and vice versa. We were both calm on the surface, but boiling beneath with anxiety. Along with all these, there were serious issues happening in my workplace, where I had to take some decision going against my Union, to fulfill the wish of the majority of my colleagues and due to this I was being branded as a villain. It is pretty much understandable that I had no mental peace. Everything just kept piling up inside me, and slowly my health started deteriorating.

I had no idea about kidney biopsy then, and I can be very much candid that, like any other person, I used to relate biopsy only with cancer. Therefore we did not go forward with the biopsy and did not visit Dr. Bijan Bhattacharya again. We did not know where to go and what to do. We would keep a regular check on my mother's health, but there was a storm brewing within us. Suddenly, one day, while talking to her sister, Jolly broke down and told her everything. That was the first time, that I had seen the surface cracking and all the emotions pouring out. For the first time we discussed amongst ourselves, and she informed me that her sister and her husband would soon visit us. Let me tell you here, that they were then staying in Haldia. My brother-in-law from his sources got us in touch with an eminent nephrologist, Dr. Arup Ratan Dutta.

On 5th April, 2002, we went to meet Dr. Arup Ratan Dutta. After seeing all the reports, he confirmed that Jolly was suffering from Chronic Renal Failure, advised a few medicines, a few more tests, and asked us to meet him after three weeks. Without much hesitation I said to him, "I am a Medical Representative. I have seen my father suffering from the same illness for years, and so both of us are aware of what can happen in the future. So it would be the best in our interest if you can explain to us everything clearly, so that we can start preparing a roadmap for the future." We wanted to be aware of the pros-and-cons and what needed to be done. With all the due respect to the doctors in West Bengal, I can very well say from my experience that the doctors cannot accept the fact that their patients or their relatives would face them and say anything knowledgeable about the illness; and therefore there remains an unassailable gap between the two. With a lot of skepticism, I spoke all the above mentioned words to the doctor. Dr. Arup Ratan Dutta replied very politely, "It is still in its earliest stage. When Creatinine touches 5 or 6 we shall do what is the best in the situation." He also said that he felt it is better to go for Kidney Transplant, than for dialysis. It would take 6-months to a year or even few years for the situation to arise for transplantation, and everything was depending on the serum Creatinine report. When asked about the expenses, what he told us, made us feel that the earth had opened up, and we had fallen into a Abhirup pit of despair! He said that the transplantation or operation would cost 4-5 lac and thereafter monthly almost 10k. All our dreams had turned into ashes. This was no more just a physical or mental struggle, with the money factor involved here; we were facing a greater obstacle. Whatever we had, was almost over, with the marriage of my two sisters, my own marriage, my father's treatment and then behind the flat. During that period, our salaries were very much mediocre, and we were building up our savings block-by-block. Jolly reported back to Dr. A. R. Dutta on 29th April, he advised her to continue with the medicines, and stay in constant touch with him.

In the meantime, after our first meeting with Dr. A. R. Dutta we prepared to fight destiny, and decided to visit Christian Medical College (CMC) Vellore, after having heard of the place from a few sources. We got in touch with the hospital via mails and they asked us to visit them on a given date.

Most probably, we left for Vellore on 12th May, 2002, reached there on 14th May, and got our appointment for the 15th. They took a few tests and a kidney biopsy. Jolly was admitted on the 17th, and for the biopsy she had to be kept admitted for 24 hours. She was discharged on the 18th, and within these 3-4 days I had pretty well understood why CMC Vellore had carved out a niche of its own. The doctors, the nurses, the support staff, the workers, all were so dutiful, responsible, disciplined, endearing towards the patients, punctuality and so on, which we had never experienced earlier. Let me give an example about the punctuality of the staff at CMC from one of the departments. On the first day after seeing the doctor Jolly was supposed to give blood for a few tests, so we had to make payments at a specific counter, from where we were told that next day sharp at 6am we had to reach a room, numbered G-20. We reached the respective place around 5.15 am, where there were already 5-6 people in the queue before us. At the front there were two local people, talking amongst themselves, which seemed gibberish to us, and the next 3-4 were Bongs, just like us. As time passed, we saw around 30-40 people behind us, but nobody from the staff around. Jolly and I started discussing that no way would the room be opened at 6 and our uneasiness was increasing with every minute. When it was about 5.50 am, among the two local people at the beginning of the queue, walked up to the G-20 room. A man opened the lock, and the woman started handing over a piece of paper with a number written on it. I was shocked to see such dutifulness, that they had already been waiting for at least an hour before the scheduled time. Not just that, even the person who was taking blood, was ready at sharp 6. We did not need more than 10 minutes to get done with it.

17th May her kidney biopsy was conducted. We were handed over all the reports in a few days' time. The reports stated that the reason for her kidney failure was Focal Segmental Glumerulosclerosis (FSGS). It was the first time that I was even hearing such a complicated medical term! With time we understood that the term meant that the reason of her kidney failure was something innate in her body, which was a Native Kidney Disease. Generally, those with Uncontrolled High Blood Pressure and/or Blood Sugar are prone to having kidney failure. In case of Jolly, neither of the two were the reasons. Jolly was thereafter given vitamins, calcium and antioxidants and was advised to 1.5 liters of fluid daily along with 50 grams of protein.

With a heavy heart and a tired mind, we returned to our City of Joy, and our everyday life resumed. Once we had decided to slog it out, we were not individuals to turn our face and run away from the scene. Our son, Abhirup, was then in the 3rd standard. To break away from the strenuous monotonous times, two of my friends and I planned for a short trip to Darjeeling, Gangtok and Pelling (small hill stations in North Bengal, in the Indian state of Sikkim, at the foothills of the Kanchenjunga Range) in December, 2002. The journey to the hill-stations provided us with extra energy and gusto, to fight the upcoming battles. The cold winds provided us with an untimely peace and gave the three of us to spend some quality time together.

Since our courtship days, both of us had pledged to meet our dreams, stand by each other and bear all the responsibilities well. We can be pretty proud in the way we had been the biggest strength to each other. Even if I had made mistakes in my life, at certain stages, Jolly never wavered. Her work ethic was immaculate. It was not in her nature to talk much, rather her actions spoke loads. She had made it her own duty, to look into the well-being of each and every family member, at times even if I would forget about my mother's check-up dates; she would be constantly at my back, reminding me. At times, when I would lose my composure while interacting with Ma, she would at a proper time make me realize my mistake. After keeping a check on her health and complications, she would strive for the betterment of each of my siblings, which she does till date. Therefore, with her initiative, my younger brother, Bacchu got married on 7th March, 2003.

As days went on to months, her Urea, Creatinine started increasing, and our trips to Vellore also went on. Accepting the physical predicaments, we planned a trip to Goa in the month of December, 2003. One of Jolly's very old bosom friend, Jacky, was then staying in Goa, who had once visited us in Kolkata years ago. It was Jolly's long standing wish to visit Jacky's house, and nobody could prevent this from happening. Once the doctors gave us the green signal, we left for Goa. In the meantime, Jolly's Creatinine was jumping by leaps and bounds, and so was Urea. Her Creatinine was above 3 and her blood pressure was pretty high. We got very tensed, and contacted the then Head of the Nephrology Department, Christian Medical College, Vellore, Dr. C.K. Jacob. He advised Jolly two medicines and urged us not to drop our plan of visiting Goa. He asked us to report to him as soon as we returned.

We visited Goa in the third week of December, and on the way back we also stayed over in Mumbai for a day. The three of us enjoyed to the hilt, although there was continuous agony and pressure building up inside me. I don't think there was much difference in Jolly's mental condition either. By the time we returned and her blood test was conducted, her Creatinine had touched 4. We contacted Dr. Jacob at CMC Vellore via E-mail, and also our local doctor in Kolkata, and the former advised us to keep repeating the blood tests regularly, once a week. By the end of January 2004, her reports showed that they were no more increasing by decimals, but by single digits. Jolly would increasingly feel discomfort and her Blood Pressure was 210/120, Creatinine around 7 and Urea much above 100. When we contacted Dr. Jacob, he advised us to start her dialysis in Kolkata, and as soon as possible to bring her down to Vellore. We decided to leave after 3rd February, which was Abhirup's birthday, on whichever day we could get our tickets via tatkal. Previously, whenever we went to Vellore, Ma would stay my siblings' house and Abhirup at my in-laws' house. This time it was not going to be a matter of 7-10 days, and there was a humongous load of pressure mounting on us. Recently, my mother would not find it much comforting to go and stay with others. Earlier her conservative mindset and ways would at times come in direct conflict with Jolly, although later on, with time, Ma became totally dependent on us. Along with all these, Abhirup's 4th standard's annual exams were knocking on the door. There were mind-boggling concerns such as who would look into his studies, his exams, his admissions to Class V and more so, whether he would be able to stay without us for the indefinite period of time. The whole expedition to Vellore would need a huge sum of money, and I had lost my sleep thinking from where I could arrange the hefty amount. One always needs some sort of belief or assurance, and in such cases I feel, the economic backbone if strong, gives a great leverage. As previously said, Jolly and I were slowly saving money, and therefore the monetary backbone was close to nothing. My other half was ill and so she would not have any difficulty in getting leave from her workplace, but what about me? Will my management allow me to be on leave for the indefinite period of time? Destiny seemed to have turned its face away from us. Where I took a lot of pride at being headstrong and gritty, I did not know whether we would be able to fight our battle alone. I was then 45 and Jolly was 37, a time when we were supposed to enjoy our daily life, spend quality time with our son, see him growing up in front of our eyes, but as I said, may be Fate did not want us to have that share of happiness. He was the Director of the script and He wanted things to take a different route. I believe we are all puppets in his Hands, and whenever, whichever string he pulls, we dance to His tunes. Here Jolly and I were dancing to his tunes of agony and despair; the whole journey thereafter, till date, has been Jolly's unwavering resolution not to accede to His tunes, and defeat Death! There is a line by a famous Bengali poet which when roughly translated stands as:

Do not abandon your journey once you have hit the road

Himalaya's snow will perspire, yet never melt!

We went about on our turbulent path with the basic idea of these lines in our mind. Both of us contacted our higher authorities and briefed them on everything, and requested them to grant us leave for the indefinite period of time. We started pondering over our options to send our son to a nearby town, where he would join a well-known English-medium school. But Jolly did not approve of this idea. We asked my younger brother Bacchu and his wife Rinku to stay in our house, along with Ma and Abhirup. My in-laws' house gave us their word to be there whenever the need would arise. I believe I have been blessed to have in-laws like them and without each of their support- be it emotional or financial, Jolly and I would not have been able to come out victorious. They stood like a gigantic banyan tree by us, and till date they are our biggest strength and confidante. In the midst of all the confusion and uncertainty, we took-off for Vellore on 4th February.

Here I shall share with you the situation at our place, on the 3rd and 4th February. As previously said, 3rd was Abhirup's birthday, and when we informed him of our decision to leave the next day, you can pretty well ascertain his condition. A 10-11 year old kid was surely facing existential crisis then! We had never had the habit of going over-the-top on birthdays, rather preferred good time on our special days, even till date. Mood was very sombre all around the house. There is a passage outside our building, and I can still remember Abhirup's face as we walked out and out of his sight. You can easily imagine the storm that must have been going on in his mind. He just stood at the gate holding on to his grand-mother, with a blank face. The young soul since then has grown into a man now, but till date he has never uttered a word as to what he felt that day. We had discussed with Abhirup about his mother's illness when he was 8years old, and since then we tried keeping him in the view of what we were deciding, and therefore he must have been prepared about what would unfold. His mother is his favorite, even till date, so it's very ascertainable what would have been going on in his mind when he saw her walking out with me. We even did not know whether there would be light at the end of the dark tunnel we were in, but in sync with our mentality, we wanted to see the end of this!

The day we left, that evening one of my very close friends from my workplace, Mr. Krishna Shankar Kundu came to me and gave me a cellphone, and said, "Take this. You will need it." Prior to this, I had never used a cell phone. Although most of my colleagues were then using cellphones, I never had one or I never saw the necessity of one. I was not willing to take it, so he almost forced me, and I will be blatantly honest here, the cell-phone was of immense help to me during the 9 months stay in Vellore. From here I began to see our near-and-dear-ones starting to stand by us. Leaving the innocent and doleful Abhirup and my ailing old mother at home and with merely 35000 Indian currencies in my pocket, I left for Vellore with my beau. Out of that 35k, 25k was my own and 10k was given by my father-in-law. Jolly's brother had just then joined a private firm, and helplessly he bid her loved sibling goodbye. Her Ma and Baba were naturally very perturbed and disturbed, and they came to bid us adieu. I'm very sure from far and near, many of our well-wishers, relatives, friends had prayed for us, and with all their love and blessings we embarked.

We reached Vellore on the 6th, and most probably on the next day we met the doctors at the Nephrology department. Jolly's various tests were conducted, and the doctors confirmed that Jolly needed a Kidney Transplant as soon as possible. They did not show much interest for dialysis and preferred straightaway the transplantation. The doctors asked us to get all the interested Kidney donors to meet them. All of a sudden, I felt a bolt from the blue striking me, and even though I knew that such a situation would arise sooner or later, I suffered a heavy jolt at that moment. I was aware of the fact that CMC Vellore always wanted 'blood-relations' to donate their organs, and legally this should be followed. CMC Vellore follows the legalities strictly. Later on, a new rule had been brought in where the spouses could donate their organs to each other, if all other criteria matched with. Jolly informed everything to her parents and siblings. Along with Jolly's sister's husband, Jolly's parents came down to Vellore on the 12th with utmost immediacy. Previously we were staying in a lodge opposite to CMC, due to certain advantages, and then we could shift to 'CMC Annex' by my brother-in-laws' constant endeavor to the Annex authorities.

13th February, all five of us met the doctors, and the doctors chose Jolly's parents and me as possible donors. Our blood tests were conducted on the 14th. The same day Jolly became unconscious while giving blood, and she had to be hospitalised. Her blood reports showed Creatinine had touched 9. Seeing her condition, the doctors started her dialysis. The next day the doctors informed us that her father had been chosen as the first choice, although his blood pressure was a bit high. He was given medicines for three days and was advised to get his pressure checked twice daily and if normal they would go ahead with the next formalities. Later on, those medicines worked well for him and his pressure was found to be normal. My father-in-law was then 65. Although 60 was the accepted age limit, he was much more healthy and fit when compared to anybody else of his age. His service in the Indian Navy and the disciplined lifestyle favored him well at this stage to gift his daughter a new lease of life.

Christian Medical College, Head of the Nephrology Department, Dr. C. K. Jacob had told us that in case donors, siblings would have a match of 70-75%, twins 100% approximately, and in case of parents it was about 50%. Listening to this, I was almost on the verge of running to Jolly's siblings, and begging them to be a spontaneous choice. Dear readers, I hope you can understand what was going over me, helplessly trying to find ways to grant my wife with a new breath of life. I pray that even the worst to worst of our enemies do not have to encounter such a situation. It was very foolish on my part to have expected that Jolly's sister who had a very small child then or Jolly's brother, who had the whole future ahead of him, could voluntarily come up to be the donor. It is a curse how the mass is very much unaware about donating kidneys for transplantation. Our body functions properly with one kidney and one can have a hale-and-hearty life. I'm pretty sure Jolly's siblings were right on their path, but I was simply helpless! I was crestfallen! The darkness at the end of the tunnel was becoming darker!

Jolly's dialysis started thereafter. I had heard later on from Jolly how agonizing it was to make a channel in her neck for her dialysis. With that began her episodes of physical pain and her extent of endurance. I have been a witness to how much pain she has gone through or seen her tolerance levels. I have merely tried to feel or empathise with her, and not been able to share her agony. Jolly had never been much vocal of her physical torment, but always being by her I could discern by looking at her face. Her eyes spoke volumes of her distress! May be, distress is a far softer a term to even describe the war!

While she was hospitalized, her dialysis went on thrice a week. I had heard from many people how painful it was and that everybody could not sustain the prolonged effects. Dialysis is an artificial replacement of the function of damaged kidneys through the process of removing excessive waste and fluids from the blood. When healthy, kidneys maintain the equilibrium of water and minerals (sodium, potassium, chloride, calcium, phosphorus, magnesium, and sulfate). Dialysis treatment replaces the function of the kidney by the diffusion (waste removal) and ultrafiltration (fluid removal). The impure blood from the body is passed through the dialyzer machine where it is purified and again passed into the body. This whole process would take nearly 4 hours, and after 10 days Jolly was discharged. Thereafter I would bring her thrice a week from CMC Annex, wait for over 4 hours, and once her dialysis was completed for the day, I would bring her back. At times, during her dialysis, I would be called to get two injections for her, one was a vaccine and the other was Erythropoietin. For my readers who are not aware, Erythropoietin injections help in the production of the Red Blood Cell, while the kidneys dysfunction. With every dialysis, the two injections were also infused. Over the three months, Jolly had to go through 36 dialysis sessions, along with the two injections and few other necessary medicines. Through dialysis the lookout was not just supplementing the functions of the damaged kidneys, but also to make the patient physically and mentally fit for the upcoming transplant. Along with this, the family members of the patient were continuously counseled upon the whole process and to prepare for the future.

We were steadily moving towards Jolly's transplantation, and on the other side various tests were being conducted on my father-in-law like Human Leukocyte Antigen (HLA), Cross-Matching, and so on. We were then provided by the hospital authorities some information about certain governmental and non-governmental social organizations that provided financial help for complicated treatment like brain tumor, cancer, kidney transplant, etc. With the help of a local Bengali person we started contacting such organizations. I had no other way, I was into a battle where I had no arms, no ammunitions, but I had set off to win the world! Very soon, I understood that Jolly's father was standing by me with the necessary financial assistance. The doctors by then had informed us that they would conduct the transplantation within a month or so, following which we would have stay for another 6 months. These 6 months would be the most crucial time where the doctors would day-to-day keep a check on the transplanted kidney and Jolly's recuperation. They even advised us to be on the lookout for some rented place, a bit isolated from the main city.

Soon we started scouting for rented places; my father-in-law and I would take off whenever we would hear of some place. Jolly was much better with the continuous dialysis, and would at times accompany us. One local Bengali gentleman, Mr. Dipankar Roy helped us to get a house, where the late Mr. Lahiri used to stay, who had come down to Vellore as a kidney patient, and thereafter stayed there permanently. It is of utmost importance here that I tell u something about Mr. Dipankar Roy, whose family along with him, since then, has become our very own and loved. It is extremely difficult to express in words how he helped us, day-in-

and-day-out at difficult times, and thereafter smiled with us during our happier times. During those days, he used to own a small hotel named *Swagatam* (Welcome), and that was where I first came upon him. Since then it's been a long endearing history.

The doctors gave the first week of March as the tentative time for the transplant and the necessary tests like Ultrasonography were all showing the right signs. From my workplace, the management deposited an incentive in my bank account, and my colleagues had collected some amount and deposited into my account. We were slowly seeing a flickering light of hope at the end of the tunnel. The saying 'Man proposes, but God disposes', has been something akin to our life, and more so ill-luck where I'm involved.

Suddenly we heard Abhirup was down with chicken pox and this disturbed us all. He had his upcoming 4th standard exams, but we could do nothing for him, except talking to him daily. To make things worse, he could not appear for the annual exams, and we became very anxious about him being promoted to Class V. On the other hand, the day we were supposed to be informed about the date of transplant, we came to know that they had found stones in my father-in-law's kidney, which was to be transplanted into Jolly's body. The doctors also informed us that they would give the next date only after they had treated the kidney, and were very sure of its condition. The doctors referred my father-in-law to the Urology department, where the doctors advised Lithotripsy treatment to nullify the stones in the kidney. Lithotripsy is a treatment by the use of ultrasound shock waves by which a kidney stone or excess calculus in the body is broken down before it is passed out of the body while urinating.

Regularly I would take him to the hospital and after Lithotripsy return with him. Since Jolly's transplant suffered a setback, her dialysis continued. The external channel on her neck had to be removed, since it could not be kept for more than a month, and then a permanent channel was set up on her wrist which was called fistula where her artery and vein were connected by surgery. During this time, we shifted from CMC Annex to the rented house of the earlier mentioned, late Mr. Lahiri's house in Sathuvachari. The whole Vellore town was formed along the lines of small hills, and Sathuvachari is a quaint little locality away from the throngs of the town. Apart from regularly accompanying Jolly and her father to the hospital, with undying energy I would keep applying for economic assistance to the various Central and State offices of the Prime Minister, President, Health Ministry, Chief Minister, Governor, Mayor and so on. I followed the same procedure with some more non-governmental organisations and in total to almost 50 such organisations. Unfortunately, I received a mere 6,500 from three organizations, where as I had to spend much more than that just to keep applying for some sort of financial assistance.

I started getting updates from back home that my well-wishers, my colleagues, my childhood friends had started going around trying to collect money from various sources. I also heard that the organization called *Katihar Prabasi Kalyan Samity* for the nostalgic people from Katihar, a small town in Bihar where I grew up, staying in Kolkata and its neighborhood, had started printing coupons and putting in their own efforts to accumulate some amount. I even heard that a few local unit of the *All West Bengal Sales Representatives Union* of which I had been an integral part in my workplace, then my younger maternal-aunt by her own efforts, Jolly's office colleagues, neighbours in my apartment and one or two friends individually had been slowly but surely making their own efforts of showing that although absent physically, they were present in absence.

Back home, in another development, Abhirup had recuperated well from chicken pox, and his school authorities had promoted him to class V. Against Jolly's wish, we decided to send our son to a reputed school in another town, a few hours from Kolkata, where his education would not be hampered. We decided that we would bring him back to Kolkata once we returned for good. With all the needed documents Jolly's brother, Abhimanyu met our son's school authorities, and with the due procedure he was transferred to the earlier mentioned school. With this, there came a huge shake-up in his life too! I became much assured about his future, although Jolly was never that positive. Miles away fighting for her new life, she was helpless, and I too was helplessly taking a step, against her wish.

Jolly's father on the other hand had been continuously fighting his own small yet most significant battle, at the age of 65. After almost three weeks, we came to know that the stones had been crushed, but they were stuck in some corner within the kidney. He was asked to flip-flap his body; regularly practice *Shirshasana* which means standing inverted on the crown of the head with the support of the arms, and there after collect the urine in a utensil. This announcement made us pretty upset, although once we returned to our rented home; we were in awe to see the dedication of a 65-year old man, getting straight to work showing his unflinching spirit to turn the tide of things, just to grant his daughter a new life. Each and every day, till today, we have been at awe of this senior citizen, how he has managed to lead a disciplined life, and everything that can never be nothing less than perfect. His hard work paid off, and the stones slowly exited the body. I have always maintained that if we could make 1000 people stand on one side and on the other my father-in-law alone, you would be flummoxed at the differences. What I'm trying to convey to my readers is that he is of a completely different pedigree when compared to any other person. His sense of 'perfect-ness' is such that he expects the same sincerity and at time exerts pressure to maintain that. There is not one daily chore he stays away from, he is what we say in Bengali- *Juto selaai theke chandi paath* which means 'from stitching shoes to chanting prayers', he is equally adept in every field. For him what he approves of, is right, what he does not, is wrong. His show of love, compassion, respect is much different to any other individual. Even at this age, he has a never-say-die-attitude, which has quite perfectly seeped into Jolly! When he is angry, he doesn't bother to consider what he is saying and to whom; does not matter even if the other person feels bad or hurt, or at least he does not show any empathy for the other person. However, it is very difficult to understand him until and unless you are around him for a long time. It is pretty accepted that if one is around him for a long time there will be fireworks, and one such episode happened in Vellore. However, with Jolly's timely intervention good sense prevailed, and post-fireworks we both have been able to tame down ourselves. Here was one lion-hearted man who gave his every drop of energy into vanquishing those stones in the kidney. Each and every day seemed like a year! Every morning I would hope to hear that the stones had left, then the next morning would hope to hear about dates for transplantation; well, I had nothing else to do than Hope! My father-in-law collected the stones and showed it to the doctors. The doctors advised for an

Ultrasonography, and the reports showed that the stones had eventually vacated the kidney. Our happiness knew no bounds. I immediately started to think that the doctors would give a date for the operation within the next few days. It was as if I had lost the rationality of my mind and forgotten all about rules and regulations. The Nephrology Department soon informed us that the particular kidney had to be kept in rest for another month, and then they would conduct another Ultrasonography to check on its functions. It seemed that the flickering candle of hope was put off as easily as it had been ignited. As usual, Jolly's dialysis continued, and my mental agony surmounted. Along with that, expenditure was crossing all limits.

My mental trauma was increasing day-by-day. Having left my ailing mother back home, 11 year old son in another town, my absence from work and to top it all my beloved's fight for survival was absolutely eating me from inside. Another thing that had been gnawing me was the economic dependence of Jolly's treatment on her father. I hated the most being submissive to somebody, for whatever purpose it might be! I had been feeling really low, and so I decided to make a trip back home, meet our son, look into what was necessary at my workplace, get my mother's pension and hand it over to her, deposit the housing loan at the right time and so on. In Vellore, just to keep my father-in-law free, after discussing with the doctors, I bought the injections for dialysis for almost two week and arranged to keep them in the refrigerator of Dialysis unit. In the third week of April I returned to Kolkata, and got down to get a few things done. Suddenly, one day Jolly called me up and informed that the doctors had decided 6th May as the date for transplant and she was to be hospitalised on the 1st. I booked a tatkal ticket in the Coromandel Express for the 30th and embarked on the journey, with the only hope that the long awaited operation would grant Jolly a new life.

1st May I reached Chennai in the evening and from there via a local train reached Vellore by 8.30 p.m. While returning to our house in Sathuvachari, my heart wanted to meet Jolly in the hospital, but I knew I could not enter her ward then, so I restrained myself. As early as possible in the morning, I went to hospital. Seeing Jolly's beaming face early in the morning, my heavy heart left a sigh of relief. She informed me that she had been taken to the Urology department where they had marked out the area of the abdomen where they had decided to adjust the transplanted kidney, and taken measurement of the interior and the exterior area, much like a tailor. Jolly also said that the doctors had begun with the preparatory measures by introducing an Immunosuppressive drug called Cyclosporine. Here, I would take a liberty to explain to my readers about two significant matters. Firstly, everything regarding transplant surgery falls under the Urology department. Pre and post-surgery treatment under the Nephrology department. Secondly, for any organ transplantation Immunosuppressive drugs are a must. Immunosuppressive drugs or medications can be explained in simpler terms as drugs that inhibit the activity of the immune system. These are used to prevent rejection of transplanted organs, treat autoimmune diseases like rheumatoid arthritis, multiple sclerosis, focal segmental glomerulosclerosis, among a few, and some other non-immune diseases like long-term allergies. Generally, such medicines are continuously prescribed to the patients. That is because, our body's Immune system will never will in no way accept an organ from another body as its own, and will rather take it as a foe. Therefore it tries to reject the foreign organ. Hence, to suppress the Immune system medicines like Immunosuppressive is prescribed. These medicines are administered after transplant to keep the organ safe, in this case the kidney; however, this makes the body an easy prey to other diseases. In all walks of life, we must maintain a discipline. Jolly was advised to have boiled water, use utensils after boiling them free of germs, abstaining from having food from outside, too see that she does not catch cold too easily, abstaining from using any washroom and maintaining cleanliness, staying away from huge gatherings and many more like these. Apart from these she had been asked to separate all her personal stuffs that she used daily. We passed 2-3 days in this manner and on 5th May my father-in-law was admitted to the hospital. From that day evening, groups of doctors from Nephrology, Urology, and Anesthesiology started visiting Jolly. Apart from them, a priestess visited her from the Chapel within the hospital campus. All the doctors explained to Jolly everything about the complexities of the operation, how long the process could take, the after-life of transplantation and more than anything infused confidence into a lady who had been looking forward to this day. Being so close at hand, few things inspired and made me look at awe, and I shall try to share it with you.

The doctors from the Anesthesiology department had come and spoken to Jolly for almost an hour. I was quite stunned to know that the doctors had done a thorough research into Jolly's life, her education, her job, her likes-dislikes, our son, his studies, my job, her father's life history, about what could unfold on the next day and so on. Later on, I had heard from Jolly that the senior Anesthetist who had spoken to her at a stretch the previous day, had stayed back on the day of operation from 7 in the morning to 3 in the evening, once she was brought out of the operation theatre.

From the Urology department, the eminent Urologist Dr. Ganesh Gopalakrishnan along with his team of doctors had also visited. Almost making us astonished, he came and spoke to Jolly about negating all the negatives and keeping faith in the Almighty. He straightaway asked her if she had been educated upon the complexities of the operation, the necessities after the operation, the disciplined lifestyle one must follow, the future of the transplant, and such peripheral stuffs. Before leaving, he said, "We as doctors shall do our duty; the rest is in His hands."

Then, the priestess from the Chapel took her turn to amaze us, having come knowing everything about Jolly and her history. She spoke to us about various matters. She then asked Jolly, "I am going to pray for you. I hope you do not disapprove?" Listening to Jolly's positive reply, she commented, "You pray to your respective God, I shall to mine." She left after wishing her the best.

Everything happening around me inspired and influenced a lot to notice the differences with things down in our region, and why thousands of people thronged to this part of our country from all over. Treatment and the whole process just do not start or end with the doctors, but there is an assortment of factors working. Mentality, intimacy, punctuality, dedication and above all their sense of responsibility was of the highest standard.

6th May 2004 was a historic day in our life! It was my darling's day of rebirth. Around 5 early morning Jolly had been asked to take bath and be ready, but going by her nature, she was ready for the D-day! More than anyone, she badly wanted this day to arrive soon. She took bath in the lukewarm water mixed with some medicated solution that had been provided by the nurses and post-bath she was given a fresh sterile gown to wear. Around 6.30 she was stretched off accompanied by two nurses and a trolley man. The nurses stopped just outside the ward and prayed to an almost lively-picture of Jesus Christ. The mood all around was such that I too felt almost suddenly some external spirit engulfing me and transcending me to a different world. Jolly stretched into the Operation Theatre around 6.45 and I waited outside, fighting pangs of agony, anxiety and helplessness. On the other hand, my father-in-law was also trolleyed inside.

Our long wait started with that. Such was my perturbation that once I would sit down, and the next moment stand-up, and again the next second I would be walking up-and-down the corridor. To ones who do not understand anything, everything is the same; but to people like me 'a little knowledge is a dangerous thing.' This is by no means a simple operation, and the whole idea of transplanting an organ from one body to another was giving me goose bumps. Although I had a lot of faith in the expertise of the doctors who would transplant thrice every week, yet my heart would not comply. Again I would go near to the OT and once at the back gate. In the meantime, without me noticing, around noon, Jolly's father had been stretched out. I came to know that post-operation, patients are brought out by the rear gate. Thereafter, started my wait near the back gate, from where I could neither go to the washroom nor to quench my hunger. What if I went for a minute or so, and Jolly is stretched out? With every passing second, minutes and hours, my patience was going for a toss. Having lost my limits of reason and patience, around 2 in the afternoon, I enquired at the Reception counter, who after a visit into the OT came back with the news that operation was over and preparations were being taken to stretch her out. This gave a little respite, and waiting outside the back gate I would run to check each time a patient would be stretched out. When the clock was just about to strike 3, I saw our much known Dr. Shanmugasundaram almost running along with a patient on the stretcher. This was the same doctor who had done my father-in-law's Lithotripsy and had taken all the measurements before Jolly's transplant. Seeing him, I found my lost courage and ran behind him asking about Jolly. He showed me the patient by him, was Jolly and signaled me to follow him. I could not believe my eyes, that the patient on the stretcher, with her face covered, oxygen cylinder by her and other monitors and equipment around, was Jolly; Within seconds, she was rushed into the Ultrasonography room in the Radiology department. I was told that they were going to conduct a Colour Doppler of Jolly. Colour Doppler is basically passing of high-frequency sound waves off circulating red-blood cells, to estimate the flow of blood through your blood vessels. Initially I thought that this was normally done after transplant, but later on I came to know that the kidney which had been transplanted into Jolly's body had not been producing urine. Dr. Shanmugasundaram informed me that post-operation situation was pretty grim, and that they were doing everything they had in their hands. I immediately felt that I fell into an abyss! Colour Doppler was over in quick time, after which, with the same urgency doctor ran into the lift, with me at his heels, and on reaching third floor, Jolly was stretched into a special room in the O3 ward, where only a few doctors and nurses could enter.

Amidst all the urgency, only Dr. Shanmugasundaram was there by Jolly's side. At that time, he was a surgeon in the Urology department. As much as I write about him, words will fall short to describe him. He had all the qualities a doctor should have while serving the society- ever smiling and always enquiring about our well-being. There had been times, when we might not have noticed him, but he came after us to enquire. I can never be able to express the extent to which he had helped us. We shall be ever grateful to not just him, but the whole set-up of CMC Vellore who gave in everything (then, now and I hope even in the future), to save lives of people.

The room where Jolly had been lodged after her transplant, patients are generally kept there under observation for 72 hours. Subsequently I had heard from Jolly that the room had glass on two walls, and from there the inmate could see everything unfolding outside, but the people from the exterior could see nothing inside. The room had just one small window through which one could interact with the patient, only at a given time.

We had been handed over a list of things that Jolly would need post-transplant, like new toothbrush, paste, comb, slippers, soap, oil, clothes and many such things which we handed over to them. The special room in which she had been kept was the O3 ward Renal Unit, from where each and every patient after transplant start learning how to live a life amongst other humans but much different as compared to them. All the education from cleanliness to having boiled water, everything is initiated from this room. My father-in-law had been lodged in a different room in the same O3 ward adjoining to the ORU. He always had the presence of his son, the youngest of the three siblings, Abhimanyu. I would also spend some time there, talking to both of them, and we decided that Jolly's mother shall not be informed about the whole thing. Around 8 we returned to our rented house, and I spent an almost insomniac night.

Next morning i.e. on 7th I reached the hospital as early as possible. I went straight to the O3 ward, but got no news about Jolly from the nurses. I started to wait outside the ORU, expecting to meet some doctors or nurses and get to know something about Jolly. In the meantime, I had met my father-in-law who assured me that he was feeling pretty well. Around 9 that morning, I saw Dr. Jacob and his team entering the ORU and after a long passage of time, once they came out I approached them enquiring about Jolly. He told me that Jolly's urine output had been pretty less, and since her transplant there had been just 50ml collected. He also told me that he could not understand what had been faltering, but they would surely give all that they had along with the aid of the Urology department. I just imagined that in all these months in Vellore, we had encountered many patients who had had their transplant, but from none had we heard of such complications. With all that I had heard and from whatever the doctors had said to me, I could gauge that the complication was nothing too ordinary. Once my brother-in-law Abhimanyu came to the hospital, I narrated to him everything, and again started to wait in hope! Suddenly I came to know that Jolly would be taken for dialysis, and such a decision in the short notice, made my heart skip a beat! With the little knowledge I had, I had never heard of a dialysis post-transplant. I knew that pretty instantly after transplant, the new kidney starts functioning properly, with there being drastic improvement in the levels of Urea, Creatinine and other factors, along with proper discharge of excessive fluids from the body. Soon I saw Jolly being stretched out, all her body covered, a mask on her face, two catheters hanging by the stretcher, other equipments, and from whatever I could see her face, it seemed to me that her face was swollen. The trolley man and the nurse beckoned me to follow them. I did not have the courage to face her, and so I stayed as much as ahead of the stretcher. More so, I did not even enter the same lift. I was very wary of the fact that on meeting Jolly's eyes I could have broken down, and then it would not have taken much for tears to roll down from her eyes either. While Jolly was being taken out of the lift, I descended the steps. I still clearly remember that it was a Friday, a day of Transplant OPD, and all other patients were by the dialysis unit. Here, on every Monday, Wednesday and Friday, post-transplant patients have their outdoor visits to the AK Lab. Meeting a few known people around, I could no longer hold back, and broke down.

Jolly was hastily taken into the dialysis unit. After four long hours she was taken out, and again taken into the ORU Unit. I again began to loiter around, and I had never felt so helpless. In the evening Jolly's mother visited the hospital to see her daughter and husband. Although she could have a perfect tete-e-tete with her husband, she could just see her daughter from the glass window on the door, but could not speak. While the other patients could walk up to the glass window and interact with their family members, seeing Jolly being unable to, gave rise to a few questions in my mother-in-law's mind. However, we tried our best not to let her know the full scenario, but

I'm pretty sure being a mother she could easily understand that her elder daughter was fighting a humongous war. The succeeding day too Jolly was taken for dialysis, which is generally abnormal since dialysis is done alternatively, and this further reinforced my anxiety about the magnanimity of the situation! I came to know that Jolly's urine output throughout the previous day had been a meager 125 ml. This meant that her kidney was still then not functioning as it should have been and therefore the situation demanded another dialysis on Sunday. That day while she was being taken on the stretcher, both of our eyes met, and my threshold broke lose. I could not control myself, and seeing Jolly's eyes wet I took my eyes off her and turned my head away. I had been very consciously avoiding such a situation all the while. On Sunday I came to know that they earlier day Jolly's urine output had increased to 250 ml. In the evening I was asked to wait back in the night and they had planned for a biopsy of the kidney. After some time Jolly was trolleyed in, and the biopsy did not take much time. A responsible lady came from the ward and asked me to wait until somebody came asking for me. It was a Sunday, and apart from relatives of critical patients, there was nobody around. It was already 8 in the evening, and after 9 I would not be allowed to wait there. More so our rented house in Sathuvachari which was quite far from CMC. I kept waiting for that man who would bring Jolly to the ward, and would repeatedly question the lady, who would every time give me the same reply, "Today is a holiday, so we have lack of staff. Please bear with us, somebody will arrive very soon." Just when my patience was going for a toss, I encountered upon another trolley man who had earlier been on duty at another ward where Jolly had been admitted before transplant. I told him about everything and he assured that he would come back as soon as the patient whom he had brought for an x-ray, would get done. I never believed that he would come since he did not have any duty for another patient from some other ward. However, stupefying me, he soon returned and took Jolly into the lift, and all along the patient he had come with, kept walking by us. The trolley man got down on the 2nd floor explaining something to the lift-man in Tamil. When we reached the 3rd floor, as I went on to take the trolley out of the lift, the lift-man himself took it till the O3 ward, and explained something to the nurses in Tamil. It was 10 already, and I started off towards our lodging.

In this respect if I do not elucidate a bit on that trolley-man it would be a great injustice, since I have maintained utmost authenticity in this book. When Jolly had been admitted for the first time, she was in the O2 ward on the 2nd floor where this trolley man was working. I never saw him seated. Even when he would have no work, he would try to keep himself busy in doing something. At times cleaning the dirt off the doors or cobwebs behind them or again arranging the trolleys and medicines or any other menial job. He knew no other language, although he understood Hindi a bit, he did not know how to communicate. Both of us would interact via sign, and whenever I would get the opportunity I would strike a conversation with him. Even outside the hospital when I had met him a few times, and had ever offered him tea with me, he had straightaway declined my offer. When I again chanced to meet the man after 6-7 years, he had retired. Quite amazingly, this time he accepted my proposal for tea.

On Monday, once I reached the hospital, came to know that Jolly was to be shifted from the ORU to general cabin of the particular ward. I was a bit taken aback thinking why the doctors had decided to shift her after giving her dialysis for three consecutive days, when her urine output had still not regularized and she had been said to be critical! While she was being taken to the general cabin, I noticed that her face and her feet were excessively swollen. Due to lack of urine excretion, fluid had been accumulating in the body. I got to know from Jolly that the swelling had reduced considerably, compared to the earlier day and on Sunday she had approximately 400 ml of urine output. On Monday, doctors from both the Urology and Nephrology departments visited her. Whatever I could understand from their discussion was that they were in serious deliberations, and were waiting for the kidney biopsy report. Such a critical situation was rarely confronted by them.

Inside the ORU the nurses had assisted Jolly in doing her daily chores. In the general cabin I decided to stay the whole day, helping her out, and in the night Jolly's mother would come and stay. Jolly was terribly weak then, so she could not have food properly, and the doctors had advised for a stipulated quantity of liquid throughout the day. As if one complexity was not enough, she was then diagnosed with Upper Respiratory Tract infection and a type of fungus in her urine. The day passed doing something or the other, talking to Jolly, and when I returned the next day, one thing seemed to have improved- her urine output had increased to 750ml throughout the previous day (Monday). I felt a bit relieved; however the doctors did not show much excitement. Only a junior doctor, Dr. Hemnath, (the then Transplant Register) gave us words of encouragement saying that things were moving towards the silver lining. His words worked wonders, and later on I understood that the doctor above mentioned had done a lot of study in Jolly's case, and therefore could have come up with such a positive response. Very soon, we saw that his words were coming true, and on Tuesday Jolly's urine output was 1750ml. Even though it was something to feel cheerful, but we were very much confused having seen the volleys of challenges thrown. I also heard that since transplant, her Creatinine which had been increasing for the past two days had been around 3. As it was a day-to-day observation scenario, I would very minutely try to notice the changes, and on Wednesday I saw that her swelling was receding. When the doctors arrived and examined, they seemed to be relaxed and hopeful. Dr. Jacob spoke to me openly- he said that since Jolly's transplant, her kidneys had not been functioning properly and therefore fluid was accumulating in her body, the reasons of which they could not perceive. They had started off with the dialysis since the nephrons of the kidney had not been functioning properly. The poor functioning nephrons gradually started working with the three consecutive dialysis that they had conducted. I have earlier said that such a critical situation was something rare to the doctors, and Dr. Jacob reiterated this to me. Since then, her urine output, Urea, Creatinine, her health conditions, and all other parameters started to improve. In the midst of all these complications, Jolly's father was discharged on Monday, and he gradually started to lead a normal life. While Jolly had been gradually recuperating from the critical complexities, another intricacy started to show. Body secretes a fluid from the point where the incision is done, which is collected in a catheter via a tube, and daily this pouch has to be discarded. Normally, this secretion happens for a week or so, but in Jolly's case, this did not stop even after a week. Due to everything, her discharge had to be deferred. Abiding by the doctors, she had to walk during the day, but it was getting extremely strenuous to do her chores with two catheters hanging by her, one to collect urine, and the other to collect this body fluid. Throughout the day I would talk to her about various stuffs, and always tried to do my bit to keep her at peace. During these conversations she would tell me that post-operation when she was getting back to her consciousness, she could hear the anxious voice of the doctors. On the first day after her operation she had been given sedatives, despite which she had intermittent sleep, and whenever she would open her eyes she would find Dr. Shanmugasundaram standing by her. Jolly further went on to tell me that she would see other patients being given normal diet, while she was not, and she could feel that her body was swelling up. During the time she was there in the ORU, she was given 6 units of blood.

After staying in the particular cabin of the O3 ward for a week, she was shifted to the O2 ward where she had been admitted twice earlier. Gradually all her complications started to normalize, yet the secretion of the body fluid did not cease. Whereas other patients get discharged from the hospital within 7-8 days, she was discharged after long, grueling 19 days, on 24th May, 2004. Incidentally, the day was Jolly's 37th birthday, and what better news to celebrate the day! She seemed to have passed the first few hurdles, and taken the first step towards a 'Rebirth'! The doctors asked us to visit them on Mondays, Wednesdays and Fridays at the transplant OPD and keep changing the drain pipe from the Urology department.

We left the hospital quite late that evening. One separate room in our rented house was left for Jolly, with new bed, bed sheets, pillows and other necessary things completely sterile. Jolly embarked on a new journey. We would visit the hospital on Mondays, Wednesdays and Fridays and meet the doctors at the transplant OPD. Without failure I would take her for a walk twice daily. On one hand the secretion of the body fluid continued, and on the other we would meet Dr. Shanmugasundaram at the Urology department to get the pouch changed on regular intervals. He was again of immense help in this scenario. Whenever we would knock on his door to get the drain pipe changed, he would leave all his work, and attend on Jolly. It also happened at times, that the pouch would spill, for which we would have to rush to the Urology department, however there too he would do the needful with a smile. At times, Dr. Karthikeyan would also lend his helping hand in this matter. You genuinely start respecting such souls, who still keep the profession so pristine. Well, it took almost a month and a half for the body fluid to cease.

CMC Vellore Nephrology department is very strict that patients must stay back at-least for 6 months post-transplant, so that they can keep a constant check on them. In the first two months thrice a week, next two months twice a week and the last two months once a week, the transplant patients are required to give blood samples and thereafter meet the doctors. We would also follow this routine, and along with my father-in-law, Jolly and I would regularly go for a walk early morning. During these walks we would meet numerous fellow transplant patients and some of their relatives. Such patients and their families were living in and around the place we were, since this area was secluded and much more peaceful than the heart of the town. With a few families we developed pretty intimate relation and it exists till date. Previously I did mention about a local Bengali gentleman Dipankar*da*, and through him we met other Bengalis like Ghosh*da*, Das*da*, Debi*da*, Banerjee*boudi*, and a few others. We would at times spend our evenings at their places, and in this way we kept awaiting for our happier days.

Over telephone we would stay in constant touch with our son Abhirup, and on listening to his depressed and morose voice we would have a hard time. I started to fear whether the decision I had taken would misfire in the future. Sitting miles away fighting a battle, we could never keep our son out of our thoughts, and knowing his condition we decided to take some steps. I decided to return to Kolkata for a few days, and meet Abhirup, and have a heart-to-heart conversation. But I could not just leave the situation whenever I would want to, because that would mean leaving behind Jolly's father to take care of all the duties. All the outdoor chores were on my shoulders, and a few my father-in-law would take care of, therefore me leaving for Kolkata would mean all the responsibilities falling upon his shoulders. After having a serious discussion among ourselves, I decided to leave for Kolkata in July, stay there for a month or two, look into our son's problems, if needed get him back to his old school in Kolkata, get back to my work for some time, to show my gratitude to the authorities who had been providing enough support to me, and then return to Vellore. Thereafter, if everything remains well, Jolly's parents could return to Kolkata, and we two souls would fight the last two three months in Vellore ourselves.

Let me now share with you a very interesting incident, which happened during the time I would accompany Jolly to the hospital post-transplant. One day while we were walking through the corridor, we saw a trio of nurses approaching. All the three were quite known to us. These nurses had been working in the O2 ward Jolly had been admitted the previous times before her transplant. As they crossed us, we exchanged pleasantries. Very soon, as we were walking away, one nurse among them called us out, came running to us and said, " Is your name Jolly Bhattacharyya?", to which Jolly replied, "Yes!" The nurse then said, "One medicine of yours has been lying in the refrigerator of our ward." Turning towards me, she continued, "Please get it soon." When I went to that ward and asked for the medicine, they handed over to me a pouch which had the medicine, and Jolly's name was written on it. This pouch contained 5 Erythropoietin injections amounting to nearly 5000 Indian Currency. This incident left me dumbfounded, seeing the responsibility and dutifulness of the nurses who remembered a medicine used almost 3-4 months earlier and had been preserved in the refrigerator. These injections had been given to Jolly during April while she was undergoing dialysis, about which I did mention earlier in this book. Within these 3-4 months numerous patients must have been admitted, numerous must have left, and many more must have had their dialysis, but the nurses had saved the right medicine and remembered the patient too. Is there any way that you do not laud the dutifulness and honesty of these nurses? Laurels will fall short if I go on appreciating our Holy place, Christian Medical College, Vellore!

Mid-July I left for Kolkata, and immediately went to meet our son in the far-off town where he had been staying. Once I met and spoke to him, I understood that he was mentally very distressed. He could not cope up with the change in the circumstances, and therefore his studies too had been falling apart. In such a situation, being stern or scolding him would make matters worse, and that sort of treatment was very much unlike to both Jolly and my ways. Abhirup has never had the habit of showing much dissent, but that night when we went to sleep, he hugged me tight and his tears gave word to his plight. His emotions broke all thresholds, and seeing him crying like a

3 year old made matters worse for me. It seemed my heart clamouring out a cry of agony. As a father I felt helpless, I felt guilty. I gauged that he had been feeling lost without the presence of his mother, father and grandmother around him. He had never till then lived without his support-systems, and clearly he could feel the absence of them above his head.

When Abhirup was in the 1st standard, Jolly fell ill, and since the 2nd standard he has been hearing everything about her illness, not understanding the magnum of it. Thereafter he has been constantly seeing our struggle and changes in our lifestyle, and coping up with that. Since those young days we were never able to buy sophisticated gifts or toys for him, or something that a child of his age would get, and quite appreciatively, he never demanded for one. He has never had the habit of nagging us for stuffs that generally a kid of his age would- chips or toffees or gifts or some toy or fast-food. I remember, Jolly bringing a soft-toy football for him when he was 15-16, saying that she always had the intention of buying something like this for him in his childhood, but due to unavoidable circumstances she could not. Currently, that ball is lodged in the showcase of his room. Even from his budding stages, he was quite aware of our restrictions and knew that sophistication or expensive lifestyle was not our cup of tea. He realized that saving money was more important than his whims and fancies.

From very early on in his life, we had always tried to educate Abhirup about life, its practicalities and its complications. At every stage in life, we have tried to counsel him and show compassion, rather than over-the-top strictness. Till date, he has never done anything to prove our ways wrong, and presently we three share a very friendly relation.

Well going back to meeting him in the far-off town, I could understand he was not at all comfortable or at peace there, and on top of that his mother's condition must have been extremely painstaking. As his parents we can now understand the effect those few months had on this kid. However, with a heavy heart I left our son in that situation and returned to Kolkata. I could not share my agony with anybody around. I rang my love, Jolly, discussed with her everything and visited Abhirup's earlier school in Kolkata. I decided to meet the Principal of The Frank Anthony Public School (F.A.P.S), and request him if he would be able to help us out and accept Abhirup back into the school. After the weekend, on Monday I visited the school and dropped my letter requesting to meet the Principal. On the second day I was able to meet him directly and I bore my heart out to him explicitly. Once I made my stand clear to him, Sir explained to me a few difficulties in admitting a student midway through a session, but eventually gave his written accent. However, here if I do not share a few things with you about his school and its Principal or the teachers, I would do a great injustice. Jolly and I have always believed in positive mentality, and that worked a lot in every step of our life. It has been our belief that if the approach is positive then the outcome will always be positive. Abhirup throughout his school-life had great teachers to guide him in almost every walk of life. The Principal, Mr. I.T. Myers has been at the helm of affairs for almost 17 years now, and he has given the school a name, fame and solidarity. So far as I know Mr. I.T. Myers is a strict disciplinarian, and that showed in his administration of FAPS. I remember, Principal Sir having even waived some sort of concession when Abhirup took re-admission, and with that he has said that since the first half of the session had been over, Abhirup would have to take the pain of finishing the entire backlog, and prepare for the upcoming examinations. I will share a small story about Abhirup's love for his school. Once while returning from Vellore, our train got late and instead of reaching our house by 5 a.m., we were late by two hours. Our son dashed into the house, and got ready within 15 minutes and reached school by 9. That day we understood that he was slowly getting eligible to sustain the pressure in the future, his love for his school, and obviously, FAPS was his *Second Home.*

Immediately the next day I brought Abhirup back to Kolkata and got him admitted to his old school. It was a great sigh of relief for him, and amidst his grandmother and uncle-aunt our old happy and smiling Abhirup was back in form. Once I informed Jolly of this news, she surely must have heaved a sigh a relief too. In strenuous times lonely away in Vellore, away from her son, she must have felt immensely at peace.

Having settled one side, I seriously got back to work, feeling guilty at my absence from the work field. I had exhausted all my accumulated leave, and was supposed to be without pay, but it was the managements' good will and helpfulness, that they did not waive my salary during those hard times. Later once I joined permanently, they decided to waive 8 days' salary per month and adjust my excess holidays. With constant pressure and nagging from my dear colleagues and local authorities, the authorities from the Head Office presented 1 lakh financial help, and this is highly unlikely of, from any private firm in the present days! Apart from this, my colleagues and a few members of the *All West Bengal Sales Representatives' Union* presented me with nearly 1 lakh rupees. The authorities from Jolly's office gave 90k, her colleagues approximately 28k, *Katihar Prabasi Kalyan Samity* 40k and the neighbors in my apartment another 40k. My maternal aunt arranged for 18k from her in-laws' and two of my childhood friends, Mr. Amal Aich and Mr. Achintya Acharya (Mintu) sent me a lump sum amount from Katihar, my childhood place. An old friend Mr. Gurudas Banerjee also stepped in with a hefty amount. Apart from the ones I have mentioned, there had been many who stood by us and helped us, and we can never forget their immense love and blessings which gave us strength to toil hard! It comes without saying that without these financial help we wouldn't have been able to steer through. However, in this case, we had such good luck that we found all such people standing by us, but in reality how many even get half of this? My in-laws stood by us through the whole ordeal, and till date they are our greatest support system. My father-in-law bore all the expenses during our stay in Vellore, and along with that he bore the extra medical expenses whenever required. Kidney transplant is such an illness where there is no full stop on expenses; expenses will cease only on the day the patient breathes her/his last. For any general public it gets extremely difficult to continue the treatment, without the support of people. As much as I say about my in-laws will be less and we shall forever remain indebted to them.

During that period in CMC Vellore a kidney transplant and all its allied expenses would amount to 3 lac and 75 thousand, including the pre-transplant 3 months of preparations and 3 months post-transplant. In our case the whole package amounted to 4 lac 40 thousand, due to the stone in my father-in-law's kidney, the extra dialysis given to Jolly and the extra days that she was kept admitted in the hospital. The 6 months that we stayed back in Vellore after her transplant including her medicines and tests every month we had an expenditure of 25k, thereafter the next one year it became 18k per month, then the succeeding three years it was 12k per month, and henceforth it became 5k per month. I had earlier mentioned that on 4th February, 2004, when we had started off for the 'war' I just had 35000 Indian Currency with me, and on 19th October when we returned victorious to Kolkata we had spent almost 8 lac. I have therefore always maintained that without the support and love of our family-friends-relatives-well-wishers we would not have been able to sail through the rough tides. I might sound bit too philosophical and preachy but I believe that during such difficult times the love and blessings offer huge strength, which cannot be compared with anything of the like.

My stay in Kolkata went about smoothly, however my heart laid in Vellore with Jolly. My mother had not been keeping too well either, so I got busy looking after her, along with the presence of my younger brother, Bachchu, his wife Rinku, and my youngest brother, Laltu, too would help as much as possible. Abhirup having come back to his pavilion was quickly settling down and coping with the extra pressure of his studies. I decided to return to Vellore in mid-September and immediately the next day Jolly's parents would return to Kolkata. As planned, I returned to

Vellore on 16th September, and my in-law's returned to their den in Kolkata on 17th.

After long and grueling 7 months, having granted a new birth to her daughter, my father-in-law and mother-in-law returned to Kolkata. Even at that age, the mental toughness and grit that they had shown, if we are able to show half of that when we reach their age, we should be fortunate. In that rented house in Vellore, Jolly and I were left to sail through the rest of the days. We would visit the hospital once a week, and all the while we had started counting our days to return home. According to the CMC rules of a patient staying back 6 months post-transplant, Jolly's term was concluding on 6th November. 19th October was the first day of the famous festival of Bengalis, *Durga Puja*. And we wanted to return home to celebrate our victory too with our family. With this intention we started trying making the doctors realize how important it was for us to return home after these 9 months of arduous journey. Nobody will ever realize the essence of *Durga Puja* in a Bengali's life, wherever he or she may be! The doctors were in no way complying to our requests, and an important reason for this was Jolly's high blood pressure, which was not settling down. After a lot of entreats, they allowed us to leave as and when we wanted to, but with an approval that we would return in December for a thorough check up. We knew it would get extremely difficult to book tickets to return home before the Pujas, so we had much earlier booked our tickets for 17th October. Having stayed in a place for 7 months, we had set up a full-fledged family, and it took a lot of time and effort to distribute some of the items to a local Bengali family, and some more we parceled home via logistics.

On 17th October we started off for Kolkata, and reached home on 19th October, thereby putting an end to the months of hardships, miseries and adversities. 19th was the *sashti*, so called first day of *Durga Puja*, and having us back Abhirup's happiness knew no bounds. He smiled and cried like a child again. There was a jump in our steps during this time, and a satisfaction that we could conquer Death, and get back victorious. On one side it was the biggest and grandest festival, and much larger the occasion with the arrival of Jolly. City of Joy indeed could be a metaphor for our family; Kolkata suddenly seemed to have an effervescent. The roads, the people, the buildings, the idols, all seemed to celebrate our victory. We were indeed ecstatic.

An altogether different lifestyle ensued thereafter. All her utensils were separated from ours, her clothes, her wardrobe, a new washroom had to be furnished for her, new shoes, nobody could enter her room after coming from outside without having freshened up, if somebody is having cold or fever they would not be allowed to enter the house or her room, if somebody would have to sneeze he or she must go out of her room or near to the window and sneeze. If there would be some guests supposed to visit we would make it a point first to enquire whether anybody was ill at their place, and if some child would be accompanying. We would not care if the guests were some of our own people, we would categorically make it a point for them to cancel their plan of visiting us with health issues, especially anything contagious. We had to turn away a friend of mine from the doorstep when we got to know that his wife had been down with chicken-pox then. Jolly has always led a very controlled lifestyle and she became much more conscious hereafter, when her only lookout in life was to live and see the days of glory of our son. Jolly had to drink 20 minutes boiled water, her utensils had to be boiled before use, restrained from having any other food from outside apart from fruits and dry items, daily morning walk, maintaining all her routine strictly and slowly getting back to normal lifestyle in sync with the rules and regulations. Along with these her medicines continued and blood tests to check her Urea, Creatinine, WBC levels every week. With every dawn was a new lease of life for Jolly and knowing her nature she was here to fight it out against the Supreme power. We slowly moved towards December, and this time we planned to take our son along with us.

We left for Vellore in December, 2004, and returned after 15 days, with all her reports perfectly normal. Out of nowhere, from March Jolly's health started deteriorating, and her reports showed incongruences. She would always feel feverish, her Creatinine kept rising and physically she felt really weak. When we contacted the doctors in Vellore, they asked us to meet some Nephrologist in Kolkata. After trying for four days, we got the appointment of an eminent Nephrologist at a private hospital. He spent almost 45 minutes talking to us, and then gave different tests amounting to nearly 10k! As we exited the hospital, Jolly promptly asked me to book tickets to Vellore, because the doctor could give us no possible self-confidence. I immediately contacted a friend of mine working with the Indian Railways, and booked a ticket in the VIP-quota. We started off for Vellore the next day. The day we reached we visited the doctors at the transplant OPD, and met the then Transplant Registrar Dr. Madhivanan, who gave us the necessary tests and asked us to meet in the evening. The tests that he had written amounted to 2k, and when the reports came out it showed unbelievable incongruences. When I went to check the reports in the evening, the doctors asked me to admit Jolly with all immediacy, and that due to excessive dehydration her Sugar showed 370, Calcium was 11, Creatinine was 2.5 and WBC was 2200. Within an hour Jolly was admitted, and I saw that the doctors had administered saline to her. When I enquired the doctors said, "We are first trying to rehydrate her, and if unsuccessful, we shall then decide what can be done." Her reports started improving magically from the next day, and the saline was continued for four consecutive days. Some other medicines were given to her, but that ceased very soon, when all her reports started to normalize with the saline being given to her. Jolly was kept for eight days under observation, and thereafter we stayed back for another 10 days, post which we returned home.

CMC Vellore generally conducts 3 transplants per week, which makes 12 in a month and 144 in a year. There are around 70-80 patients each day of an OPD, which means approximately 200 in a week. I don't think even the best of the Urologists in Kolkata get to transplant so many patients or even the Nephrologists get to see post-transplant patients. I feel the expertise of the doctors in CMC, Vellore, handling these numbers of patients, brings to the table the difference in quality and their success ratio. Of late a government hospital and a few private hospitals in Kolkata have been conducting kidney transplants and post-transplant check up pretty well. I believe post-transplant check-up is equally critical, due to which CMC Vellore makes it a point for patients to stay back 6 months after their transplant.

In 2005 we visited CMC Vellore twice-once in June and again in December. Thereafter, from 2006 to 2014 we would visit once a year, and during this time apart from a few a menial issues, there was nothing too disturbing or challenging. Immunosuppressive induced issues went on, for which every 2-3 years doctors regularly altered them.

In 2004, once we returned from Vellore Jolly left her job and this was with a larger purpose in mind. For a home-maker it becomes very cumbersome to maintain her health post-transplant, her job and her familial responsibilities her way and there are certain constraints. Even when we would be around to help her, Jolly would always want to control the reign and do things her way. Jolly would always say, "I have been granted with a grace life, and I shall present this lease of life for my family, and more so for my son." Jolly left her job to sculpt a good upbringing of Abhirup. Jolly surmises that since she had taken up the reigns in her hand and looked after Abhirup's overall development she was able to keep him going strong. As Muhammad Ali spoke, "Don't count the days, make the days count" and Jolly believed she could 'make her days count' giving her soul and body for her son, whose future was everything she looked forward to. We accept that his mother has been playing the most important role in his life since then. When we returned from Vellore, and Jolly took everything in her hand, she could understand that it would need a lot of time and energy to rebuild Abhirup and his personality. At that crucial juncture she believed a mother's role becomes very important and therefore whatever decisions she took, our son vindicated it in his Board results. All the financial responsibilities fell on my shoulders thereafter. It became very difficult but as I have always said, self-belief and blessings of your well-wishers helps you to sail through, and with that my positive mentality played a huge role to carry forward.

On the other hand, my mother's health worsened, and suddenly in 2008 her left side was left paralyzed after a massive stroke. After consulting specialist doctors, her treatment went on at our home, and we kept attendants 24 hours to assist her in her daily work. We did not get preferred results, and she developed bed-sore due to constantly lying on the bed and no movement at all. Jolly could not do much because she would then be easily prone to infection, yet she did as much as she possible. I even tried continuing Ma's treatment from some nearby relatives' house, but being unable to do so, we admitted her to a nearby hospital. She fought her small battle at the winter of her life for 59 days, and eventually on 11th September, 2008, Ma breathed her last. There are a few people who throughout their life face hurdles and are bereft of happiness, and my Ma was one of them. I wanted to give her a share of peace and happiness during the winter of her life, but that too I failed miserably. I was so busy fighting adversities that I feel I could not offer her the time while she was slowly crumbling down, although I'll tell that I did put in the effort as much as I could. Relentlessly struggling through the years, age was catching up too soon, and with that I was losing all my patience; there was certain uneasiness and dissatisfaction which got exhibited on my near-and-dear-ones, and often it would be Ma on the receiving end. At this stage when it's been 9 years since she has left me motherless, guilt engulfs me but I cannot go back and erase those bitter memories!

Ma used to sing beautifully, especially *Rabindra Sangeet*. It was she who sowed the seeds of my interest in poetry and recitation, and even my first mentor and teacher. During her last days, she would often request me to recite a few of her favorite Tagore poems. I remember vividly from my childhood, that Ma would make creative designs with cotton, and then stuff them into fat-mouthed glass bottles which would look exquisitely aesthetic. Under familial responsibility and pressure, she dumped all of that into oblivion. Whatever little I have been able preserve and hone my skills in recitation, I'm indebted to my mother for having made me fall in love with poems. In fact, our son too later on showed interest in vocal music, and has been learning Indian Classical music along with lighter forms since he was 15-16.

When Abhirup was 6, he first experienced the death of his Dadu and then the death of his Amma when he was 14. By the time he was 10 or 11 he had already learnt everything about his mother's illness and we had made him quite prepared for the worst, since transplant patients have a looming uncertainty over them, as they are so fragile. However, we always tried to put into his thinking that with positive approach and belief in one's own self, many unimaginable battles can be half-won. As he grew up we saw hints of these teachings sprouting its fruits, and with every class he started to improve. *'To be or not to be'* was no more the question, rather 'what to be' was. In 2010 and 2012, Abhirup against all expectations came out with flying color in his 10th standard board exams (Indian Certificate of Secondary Education- ICSE) and in his 12th standard board exams (Indian School Certificate, ISC), scoring 86% in both. In class 12 he scored 94 in English, and at last he could give wings to his ambition to study English Honors, when he got admitted to the reputed Asutosh College, affiliated to the University of Calcutta.

Generally when people would be crest-fallen at such battles being thrown against you, we never allowed ourselves to be bogged down. We would still make our attempt to smile and what better than a change in weather or environment. We were never short of oxygen to live, and so our 'elixir of life' was the three of our love and attachment. In 2008, we made a trip to Kalimpong, Lava, Lolegaon, in 2010 we went to Vizag, Araku Valley in Andhra Pradesh, and then in 2013 to Shimla, Kulu, Manali in Himachal Pradesh. Therefore you can perceive that for us living each day together and with the idea to make the most of the time in our lives was ultimate.

FAR FROM BEING OVER

Life is very unpredictable, and as the saying goes, '…when God gives, he gives in abundance", He gave us in abundance joy and memories to cherish since Jolly's rebirth. However 2015 had a different story to tell and a sudden twist again gave us nightmares and another visit into the dark lanes of struggle and agony. Three years just whizzed past and Abhirup was appearing for his Third Year Honours exams in April, 2015. Since we were awaiting his completion of examinations to go to Vellore for Jolly's annual checkup, we booked our tickets for 11th May, 2015. We decided against Abhirup accompanying us, since his various admission examinations for Post-graduation in English was slated all over India at various Universities during the period. We reached Vellore on the 13th and like always, various tests were conducted. What we would usually do is, we would meet the doctors for three consecutive OPD's and then return to Kolkata within maximum two weeks, and this was nothing different. Since we reached on a Wednesday, we planned for Jolly's OPD on Wednesday, Friday and Monday and then board the return train on 19th May, Tuesday midnight. It was then, that all hell broke loose, and we were faced with another chapter of agony and scramble for survival. This episode was far more hellish, intricate and demanding than the previous, because here it was just the two of us battling it out. In this battle we were totally at our wits end. It was quite unbelievable that at the end of those six months I could return home with Jolly by my side. This I believe could only happen because of the paramount patience, expertise, dedication, knowledge about the diseases, and never-say-die-attitude of the doctors of various departments at CMC Vellore, especially the Nephrology department. Along with that, the love, blessings and prayers of people back home, who have constantly stood by us, and obviously Jolly's unflinching perseverance to defeat Fatality!

As I have earlier said, we reached Vellore in the early hours of Wednesday, and after a siesta of two hours, we reached the transplant OPD by 7.30. Following the regular procedure, we met the doctors and then gave blood and urine for tests. For the very necessary 24hours Urine/Protein test we collected the container to collect the urine. As usual, I came in the evening to check Jolly's reports and they were all normal. For some reason, Jolly gave her 24-hour Urine on Friday, and this report showed a huge anomaly- 8 times of the normal level, and seeing this anomaly the doctors advised for a re-test which showed similar result as the previous. However, on 18th Monday, after OPD the senior doctor, Dr. Basu Gopal said to Jolly, "Urine and Protein ratio levels staying high is extremely dangerous. You might stay fit as of now, your Creatinine levels will stay within limits, but if you leave now, in the recent future your Creatinine levels will shoot up and then it might get extremely perilous to tackle the situation. Surmising the kidney shall then move towards rejection and thereby making conditions extremely hazardous. Therefore it is our opinion that you defer your return as of now and your treatment must start as soon as possible." When we enquired about the type of treatment, they said, "Initially, we will begin the biopsy to locate the problem or reason and then take the next step." We were crest fallen, but having nothing in our hands, we cancelled our tickets and informed Abhimanyu of the change in plan, and later spoke to our son too.

Thursday, 21st May Jolly was admitted to the hospital, and within a few hours her kidney biopsy was conducted. In few days after waiting anxiously her reports came out, where it was stated that there was a growth of antibodies in her system, which were attacking the transplanted kidney and if this carried on for a longer period, it would lead to the rejection. Therefore the doctors decided to start with the treatment which was called plasmapheresis. I had never heard of such a medical term, and I just stared blankly at the doctors and enquired more about it. They explained saying, "Through transfusion of Plasma or Albumin via a machine, new antibodies would be produced into the body, and for this process would need her to get admitted for 15 days. The whole process would require 6 courses of transfusion, every 1-2 days gap between two, and it would amount to 4 lac approximately." If one is ailing, the plasma carries antibodies that attack the immune system. A machine is used to remove the affected plasma and replace it with purified plasma or a plasma substitute. This is also known as plasma exchange and the process is similar to kidney dialysis. Plasmapheresis has been used to assist the patients who have gone through organ transplant to prevent the body's innate rejection process.

As I heard of the amount and the extensive process, I felt I was getting sucked into a pool of quagmire and I lost all my senses! My body became numb, and I could not bring myself to believe what I had heard! We had come with maximum 50k, which was dwindling away, I had taken leave of 10 days, which had already exceeded by 5 days, and now we were stranded in between another challenge! The famous Bengali euphemism *chokhe shorshe phool* which means 'unspeakable disaster' keeps coming back to my mind. Trying to control our disbelief and ill-luck, when we questioned the doctors about the success-rate of the treatment, they said, "There is no certainty over the result of the treatment, but at this moment there is nothing better than plasmapheresis either."

After returning to our lodge we detailed Jolly's brother Abhimanyu about everything and then decided on the next course. Over the phone, he asked us to go ahead, and without any hesitation he assured to provide all sorts of financial help when the need be.

27th May Jolly was admitted and I informed the doctors that I would not be able to give more than 25k at that moment. The doctors gave me in writing that we could pay the bill weekly as per the expenditures. Without wasting much time, the doctors got Jolly ready for the first of her six courses, and made a channel on her neck. We were informed that

116

she would be taken to the dialysis room for her first course of plasmapheresis treatment. Since I had no knowledge about the whole process, I was extremely tensed and worked up! However, I don't remember Jolly being one bit perturbed on the surface, since she believed the doctors at CMC could do nothing wrong. Although I too believed in this, however at that moment I was shell-shocked and everything seemed deplorable or terrible.

The clock went well past 10 at night when Jolly was taken into the dialysis unit for her first course of plasmapheresis. Having waited since the evening for this, I became extremely impatient and agitated, because I could not stay back after 9 p.m. I had wanted to stay till she had been shifted to her bed, ask her about how she was feeling and then leave for the lodge at Sathuvachari. However, this did not happen, and I left after she was taken into the dialysis room, fretful and apprehensive. Somehow the night passed, and when I went to meet her in the morning she was still asleep. Once she woke up, she informed me that she had returned the earlier night around 1.30. When I enquired about the delay in previous night's preparations, I came to know that the whole process needed a unique type of dialyzer machine, some unique arrangements and a specialized technician, and since it was the first day, they took some time to set-up the whole thing. In the first phase, the doctors conducted Jolly's plasmapheresis consecutively for three days. Once she would be brought back to the ward, the doctors would administer IVIG (Intravenous Immunoglobulin) transfusion that would go on for approximately four hours. According to the needs, at times IVIG transfusion would be given more than once a day. Due to these, Jolly's whole routine got shuffled, and she started developing certain health irregularities. Post the second dose of plasmapheresis, Jolly started developing allergies all over her body for which medicines had to be started. Since the third dose, situations worsened- Jolly started having acute diarrhea, Urea, Creatinine, WBC, Platelet count, Sodium, Potassium, Hemoglobin, Sugar, Lipid profile and all other parameters showed extremities. Medicines even did not render positive results and my agony soared! At this stage, Jolly's food intake too stuttered to bare minimum. Under a lot of medications, she was given a break of three days, after which she was given her fifth plasmapheresis under very difficult situations. Situations worsened to such an extent, that Jolly literally fell at the foot of the technician pleading to stop the fifth course, mid-way, experiencing an inexplicable discomfort in her body! During the plasmapheresis that day, Jolly had excessive loose motion during the process! For a patient as weak as Jolly this was deplorable, but for me as an onlooker (more so, her husband) was furthermore agonizing. Again, the situation had come, where I could do nothing to help my my beloved out of this situation, other than just being by her, helplessly looking at her, and at times caressing her forehead. Seeing her weakening state the doctors decided against the sixth plasmapheresis. They said that they had earlier known of mere reactions to the plasmapheresis, but the intensity of the reaction on Jolly was quite extreme. In place of her previous Immunosuppressive medicine the doctors initiated a new medicine called Tacrolimus. Thereafter, she stayed in the hospital for a week, and once her condition improved slightly she was discharged.

It has always been so that at crucial stages of my life, I have found the support and presence of people who have provided me with the extra mileage to fight on. During this period too, I found the presence of one such local Bengali family, whose continuous support provided us with energy and food for the body and soul. During this period while Jolly was admitted in the hospital, except their rice, she could not eat any other dishes provided to her. Although a lover of South Indian dishes, this period she did not like any of the items given by the hospital, due to the poor gustatory perceptions. There was no option of me cooking anything from the lodge, since the whole day I would be at the hospital, and I am not much of a cook. To avoid such difficulties, I would get one fish fry and a lentil soup for Jolly, to have with the rice, from *Banerjee Hotel*, opposite to CMC. The owner of the shop, Banerjee*boudi*, was an old acquaintance of ours, whose husband too was a kidney transplant patient, and had passed away four years earlier. I believed that whatever I would get from her hotel would be absolutely perfect for any transplant patient. She would, with a lot of care and responsibility, prepare the fish fry and the lentil soup with some vegetables in it for Jolly, which she would eat happily. I too would have my lunch and dinner from the same hotel, and soon it would be this that Banerjee*boudi* would decline to take money for either Jolly's food or mine. I'm very much against such practices, but I knew she was doing this out of love and care for us, and I felt extremely uncomfortable to buy anything from there later on. Those six months that we stayed in Vellore, Banerjee*boudi* would not charge a single penny from me, to whatever we bought. Her daughter Mampi, would often visit Jolly at the hospital. We can never forget the beneficence of the two lovely souls in being a pillar during our crumbling days. Unfortunately, in the late 2015, Banerjee*boudi* sold her shop, and along with all the workers returned to her home in the suburbs of Kolkata, a village almost 70 kilometers from the City of Joy. Later on, from January 2017, they reopened their hotel at a different location, but in the same locality. We have always been grateful that we found the presence of such people during our days of pain and suffering, and such beautiful souls touched us with their humanity, bringing smiles to our faces.

Gradually, Jolly started recuperating and all her reports started to show improvements. Acute diarrhea had ceased and according to the doctors through the plasmapheresis they had been able to prevent kidney rejection. After another week or so, on 22nd June we quite adamantly returned home, very much against the doctors' wishes. They wanted us to wait back for 10 more days, but we were helpless since we wanted to return to take decision on our son's admission for Masters. Along with that I had already exceeded on my sanctioned leave.

As soon as we returned, Jolly's Creatinine started increasing by leaps and bounds, and along with that her diarrhea too. However, we hoped that it would cease in a course of time, and tried to keep it out of our head. In June, Abhirup's graduation results were declared, and he scored pretty well. He started applying at various universities all over India, and eventually got selected at the prestigious Pondicherry University (Central) in the Department of English and Comparative Literature. Meanwhile, Jolly's Creatinine kept rising, and her diarrhea did not cease. When we contacted the doctors at CMC, they asked us to return to Vellore with immediacy. We were extremely confused at this stage, since our son had never wanted to leave this city, and had he waited for some more time he would have surely cracked the University of Calcutta entrance examination, but that would mean taking a risk, of leaving the opportunity at a Central University. After serious deliberations with his Ma and Mama Abhimanyu, we decided on Pondicherry University, since that would mean him staying close to Vellore, and Abhirup would also gain experience of staying alone, taking care of his things by himself, which would surely benefit him in the future. I contacted the authorities at my workplace and they assured me of providing any sort of assistance. Therefore another quantum shift took place in our life, when we three decided to leave together for Vellore on 5th July, and 8th was Abhirup's admission at Pondicherry University. We decided to leave for Pondicherry from Vellore before dawn on 8th, so that we could reach University by 10 a.m., and then return the same night, while Jolly would meet the doctors alone at the OPD. As planned we left on 5th July from Kolkata, and reached Vellore on 7th, around 4 A.M. Abhirup and I left for Pondicherry on 8th at 5 a.m., reached our destination by 10, once the admission procedure was completed and he was allotted his hostel room, we started our journey back to Vellore, only to reach our lodge around 11 p.m.

Abhirup's classes were to commence from 19th, which would mean he could stay with us for 10 more days. In Vellore, the doctors advised Jolly for a kidney biopsy. The doctors doubted a relapse of kidney rejection. To prevent kidney rejection high dose of Methyl Prednisolone 1 gm. injection was initiated along with medicines for diarrhea. During her Plasmapheresis, she had been given Methyl Prednisolone which shot up her blood sugar levels. To keep her sugar in check, the doctors administered insulin, but her diarrhea was not responding positively to any medication. Seeing this, Jolly felt that the hospital food was not suiting her and she expressed her feelings to the unit head, Dr. Santosh Varughese. In virtue of her request, the doctor started another dose of antibiotics and discharged Jolly.

Let me tell you here that we knew Dr. Santosh Varughese very well since his youth, when he was a junior doctor in the unit where Jolly had had her transplant. Therefore, we were very familiar to him. From our earliest days in CMC, Dr. Santosh has been one of the few people who have stayed till the present. He is currently the Head of the Nephrology department, Unit 2. Therefore we had wanted an expert advice from him once the doctors had decided for the Plasmapheresis. He was on a long-term leave then, and I contacted him over Facebook introducing myself and all that had been happening. He immediately replied affirming Plasmapheresis, saying that in the present situation it would be the best way forward. He even wished Jolly the best.

Jolly's situation did not get any better once she came back to the lodge. Her health deteriorated, she fell extremely weak and fatigued, her Urea, Creatinine shot up and WBC stooped to a new low! Her appetite suffered a heavy jolt due to all this! Within months a full grown, green tree had shed all its leaves and looked famished, broken and withered. Life is cruel, I believe, to torment souls such as us. The doctors even suggested for a Colonoscopy, but we were always trying to defer it, because it is physically very painful and traumatizing. Seeing the worsening conditions, the doctors were always on their toes!

While all this was going on, I accompanied Abhirup to Pondicherry and once he was settled, the same evening I returned to Vellore. The lodge again looked empty- as empty as a street on a strike or a forlorn road on a sweltering scorching afternoon. The time that he was here, it gave us a homely feeling. This would be the first time that he would be staying away from us for a long period of time. Although we knew we had prepared him well enough to take control of his life at such junctures, still that feeling of not being able to see your kid around leaves a very Abhirup pain in the heart! Once he left, he marooned us two souls, alone, but no, we did not lose the courage or accept defeat. We were ready again to see the end of the tunnel. We were prepared to meet fatality eye-to-eye, and reverse our adversities.

Almost with their backs against the wall the doctors decided against our wish to conduct a colonoscopy on 4th August. The reports did not show much, other than 2-3 lumps in her colon. However, the colon tissue biopsy reports showed the presence of CMV (Cytomegalovirus) infection. This infection is often found in the blood of transplant patients, and this is highly dangerous. The expense of this treatment is also huge. Earlier CMV was tested negative whenever it was done, but this time since it was found in the colon tissues, the doctors assumed it to be the reason for diarrhea. The doctors immediately started an antiviral named Ganciclovir injection- one daily for one month continuously. Each injection would cost 2200 Indian currency. They had to be collected from the hospital pharmacy and administrated from the 24 hours injection room at same time every day. It seemed the silver lining behind the dark clouds would never again shine in our favor. Having immense trust and belief in the doctors, we did whatever the doctors asked us of. The transplant OPD staff accepted to keep the injection in their refrigerator. I decided that I would buy 5 at a time, so that it won't be a problem on weekends or holidays when the office would remain closed.

Suddenly a news from home reached us, which shattered our heart into pieces, and personally for me it became doubly-distressing. During our last visit in June, while Jolly's plasmapheresis was going on, I came to know that my younger sister, Gopa, who is two years younger to me, was having a rough time with a tumor on her back and the doctor had asked for an immediate operation. The orders were followed and later we came to know from her husband that the tumor was malignant. The news started gnawing into my skin and it left both Jolly and me devastated. We felt really helpless knowing that we could not be by them or be of any assistance during such a time. There has always been a very friendly quotient between my sister's husband Golok and me, and we have stood by each other whenever there has been a need, thereby we have struck a great understanding and brotherhood. But during their adversities, not having me by him, he would often express his agony, and sitting miles away I could just live in despair, praying for their strength. In Kolkata, they met the concerned doctors and Gopa was given 6 rounds of Chemotherapy. Along with the medicines, Gopa recuperated pretty well and slowly achieved normalcy, but I knew I would have to live my whole life with the regret of not being present with my sister and her family during their times of crisis! You know what, it was their 25th Anniversary while they were fighting to make things work, and find their share of light at the end of the tunnel! This is Fate being Cruel!

Now coming back to Vellore and Jolly, a central channel was made on her neck for the Ganciclovir injection. Every Monday, Wednesday and Friday we would go for the OPD in the morning, and in the evening around 4 for the injection, which would be given along with saline for 60 minutes. Rest of the 4 days also we would similarly go in the evening and Jolly would be given the injection. Slowly this routine became extremely rigorous and took its toll on both of us. On the days of OPD, the clock would strike 3 p.m. by the time we would finish our lunch, and by 4 we would again be at the hospital. The rigors of this routine took its toll on Jolly, and after 16-17 days she could not make herself to get up and do her duties. She would dictate me and I would somehow prepare boiled rice and one vegetable dish and somehow gulp it down. Diarrhea seemed to have decided not to cease, rather situation worsened to such an extent that she could not even walk a few steps. I could easily perceive that just because it was Jolly, she could carry on doing her work under such discomfort. This again proved to me her mental strength- this strength isn't something she consciously develops or developed, but it's been innate in her, which at such junctures spontaneously charges up! It's not easy to maintain one's patience and keep control over emotions, therefore it so happened that I would be rude with Jolly at times, and once I even lost my cool and behaved rudely with a doctor.

Seeing her crumbling day-by-day, I expressed my concern to the transplant registrar, Dr. Goutham, "Let Jolly be admitted as soon as possible and continue her injections, because it is getting extremely difficult for her to travel everyday to-and-fro between lodge and hospital." The doctor agreed with me, did not waste any time and immediately admitted her.

In an hour or so, the senior doctor, Dr. Kakade Shailesh Tulshidas sounded his concern and anxiety seeing Jolly's pale face. The doctor with utmost immediacy started medications and gave some directives to the nurses. Even before her reports came, the doctor started Sodium bicarbonate IV injection through a special device, on the basis of the doctor suspecting a drastic fall in Jolly's sodium bicarbonate. When the reports came, it proved what the doctor had suspected- Jolly's bicarbonate was 8, whereas 22-29 is the normal level. Seeing the reports Dr. Shailesh remarked to Jolly, "How could you pick yourself up from the lodge and come till here? In this stage a patient loses their consciousness and collapses. You have come here at the right time or else things could have complicated further!" Along with this, her Creatinine, Hemoglobin, WBC and a few other parameters were off the mark. After 25 Ganciclovir injections, seeing no improvement, they ceased it, and all the while they tried to normalize her distorted parameters. Along with this, they conducted her Endoscopy, repeated Colonoscopy, Lung X-ray, Lung Biopsy, Bone-marrow test, and also her blood, urine and stool test. The doctors kept on trying to determine why her parameters and diarrhea was not coming under control. Her Endoscopy, Colonoscopy and Bone-marrow tests did not show much incongruity, but chest x-ray showed a major issue, and to detect it they conducted her lung biopsy. The reports showed reasons for concern, and it became furthermore complicated when she had hemorrhage during her lung biopsy. This made the senior and the junior doctors run helter-skelter, and Dr. Shailesh took turns to show me the picture of the biopsy of her lung, and their reason for concern. What I saw was her left lung looked totally black! I was taken aback because a fortnight back the reports were all fine. When I showed my disbelief, and from my little knowledge I enquired, "What are you expecting this dark patch to be, Pneumonic or Tuberculosis?" The doctor replied, "If that is the case treatment is available, but we doubt it to be a perilous fungal infection, which can be extremely fatal!"

I have mentioned for numerous times throughout my book about the intimacy and dutifulness of the doctors, staff and nurses at CMC. Therefore, I cannot restrain myself from putting my hand into the memory-box and bringing out another story for you. During this period of Jolly's life-threatening infections, we were missing Dr. Santosh Varughese, who was nowhere to be seen. Unable to withhold my curiosity I asked junior doctor, Dr. Athul Thomas one day, and he said Dr. Santosh was then out of India. He knew of our proximity to Dr. Santosh Varughese, and so he said, "You have nothing to be worried, because we are regularly in touch with him, and decide on the course of action only after discussing with him. We send him all your reports via e mail, so you can be rest assured." He further added that Dr. Santosh would return within 2-4 days. Jolly's lung biopsy was done on a Friday, pulmonary hemorrhage and effusion occurred, and under the directives of the Pulmonologist she was given oxygen. The nursing in-charge advised Jolly to be shifted a bed nearer to the nurses' cabin, so that they could keep her under constant check, especially at nights. Two days later, on Sunday, around 8 in the evening while Jolly was getting ready to have her dinner, Dr. Athul came and said, "Hold on, your friend is coming!" Around 8.30 we saw, with a small bag slung on his shoulder and one in his hand, Dr. Santosh Varughese walked in. He kept his bags on the nurse's table, and straight walked by Jolly's bed side and said, *Nomoshkar.* Then he spoke to the doctors for over half-an-hour, giving them directives regarding the future steps. Then he turned to me and said, "There must have arisen a few doubts in you regarding Plasmapheresis and its effects, which is pretty much accepted and it's inevitable. Post-

Plasmapheresis few reactions are seen, but in Jolly's case whatever has happened is unexpected and unfortunate." Previously I had expressed my concern and dissatisfaction regarding plasmapheresis to a few doctors, and listening to him I could estimate that Dr. Santosh was well aware of my emotions. So coming back to why I brought up this topic, is that four days prior to everything stated above, Dr. Santosh had been conferred with the title of MRCP from the *Royal College of Physicians*, London, which I came to know much later from his Facebook account. But I was bemused by the fact that he had come straight to the hospital from Chennai airport, travelling from America, that too on a holiday around 8.30-9 at night. It was not a mere visit, but he spent enough time with the patient and her family with a smile on his face. This was implausible for a common man like me and I shall cherish these moments of happiness, for people like Dr. Santosh who have maintained the ethics of the profession to its core. It is for people like Dr. Shanmugasundaram, Dr. Santosh and more others, like them from various departments that patients from all parts of India flock to CMC Vellore. You cannot but believe them to be incarnation of God for people like us.

Well the situation with Jolly became from bad to worse. Everyday various bacterial, viral, fungal, worms, gastrointestinal infections were found in her body and thereby different medicines were administered. Her body had become a breeding ground for infections like cyclospora, microsporidia, and the most fatal fungal infection Nocardia too! In such a situation, you can easily understand mindset wavers, and physical pain supersedes everything. An exemplary person of positive mindset and mental strength too became weak to sustain the extreme physical pain, and cried out to Dr. Athul Thomas, "I cannot take it anymore. Please let me leave. If I can live the rest of my life on dialysis that would be great!" These words uttered by her showed how much pain she had been undergoing. We all knew Jolly would be the last person to lose all her hopes and belief. Even the junior doctor said, "Such a conscious and sensible patient like you are telling me this? Everything has been detected, and now it's all about the right medicine, which has also been initiated."

This phase was extremely strenuous and tough for me, because I had nobody to fall back upon. I could understand the pressure of the storm that had been passing over us, and at times I would badly want Abhirup to be by me. He was having his classes, and almost every weekend he would travel from Pondicherry to Vellore, spend the two days with us, and return for classes early morning on Mondays. For me, his presence would be a welcome relief, and in-spite of the numerous perturbations about my job, my salary, the expenses in Vellore, and more than everything else the need of taking financial assistance from Jolly's brother, Abhimanyu, I would spend those two days with him. Although Abhimanyu had never thought twice before lending his helping hand for his loved and mother-like eldest sister, I was always wary of the fact of being in debt, since this was such a debt which even in the next 10 lives we would not have been able to repay!

There are small stories without which this book will remain incomplete, because somewhere down the line this book narrates the struggle of a kidney-failure patient in Jolly, her battle internal and external, my battle as being the person nearest to Jolly, and of course Abhirup's, who has been seeing everything unfolding since he was 8 years old. So, one day while his mother was battling it out against the infections and bacteria in her body, his maternal aunt called him up, and told him that Jolly was critically ill, and it was paramount that he travels down to be by his father. On one such weekend, he travelled down and straight came to the hospital. I was sitting outside the ward where Jolly was admitted. He came to me very anxiously and enquired what had happened and narrated to me what his maternal aunt had told him. It had become a habit for Jolly to call him every night for few minutes and Abhirup would categorically enquire how Jolly was doing. Even when it was the worst and reports were going haywire, Jolly would not indulge much into the nitty-gritty of the reports to him. She had not told him about her breathing troubles and the diarrhea which had been recurring.

The day he came, the doctors had the earlier night informed me about the dark patch in Jolly's left lung and its possible reasons! So when he arrived, I came out with him, sat down on the chairs outside, and explained the whole situation. Since the days when he would understand Jolly's situation, I had made him feel that her life was always on the basis of the present and we should always be prepared for the worst. Some skeptics might term me as pessimistic but this was making us prepared for anything that can strike patients like Jolly who lived their life on the edges, as anything could happen! Therefore, Abhirup on understanding the seriousness of this situation, asked me how bad it was, and I told him with a lump in my throat that the doctors had asked us to be prepared for the worst, if the black patch showed the worst! Abhirup was then 21, and I'm sure he must have felt a surge of disbelief, but he never fluttered once. Thereafter, he had even seen his Ma soiling her clothes, when she did not even have the energy to get up and rush to the washroom. During that journey I could understand the agony he was facing inside him, when he left in the early hours of Monday, leaving behind his bedridden mother waging a battle against the forces! The previous evening he met one of the junior doctors, Dr. Athul, and enquired from him about Jolly's condition. Dr. Athul categorically explained the whole scenario to him, assuring him that the doctors would give their best efforts to bring back his mother to her earliest state. Although the doctors had given more than 100%, Jolly's mental strength was also a great reason for her to have been victorious in this battle. But there forever looms large a question- how many times can the body and the kidney bear the brunt and not succumb?

Anyway, according to the need, varieties of antibiotics, anti-bacterial, anti-fungal, antiviral, antihelminthic drugs like Cotrimoxazole, Ciprofloxacin, Ceftadizime, Meropenem, Ipipenem, Co amoxiclav and Albendazole were given to her. Meropenem IV injection was given for 14 days, post which Ipipenem IV injection for another 14 days and Ceftadizime IV injection was also given. Along with these, three types of oral Antibiotics/Antibacterial and Albendazole too. She also had to be given 2 units of blood. For different blood tests, administering of Intravenous (IV) injection and blood transfusion, needle had to be pierced on her arms for countless number of times, leaving her arms swelling and blue-black with blood clots. Even after having suffered to this extent, there were no signs of improvement, rather her reports showed surge further down. Her WBC touched the pit, her three months prolonging diarrhea did not control and she had become as frail as a flower. She always needed somebody at her bedside to assist her round the clock. When the doctors came on their rounds on the morning of 19th September, Dr. Anna T Valson came on her rounds and said to me, "Jolly has become highly immunosuppressed, i.e. her immunity against infections has acutely minimized, where by opportunist infections have attacked her body leaving her wrecked. Jolly's life is our priority and therefore we are contemplating of stopping her Immunosuppressive medicine!"

From 20th September her immunosuppressive drug was ceased, and inevitably all her reports slowly started to improve. Diarrhea too seemed to have been getting better, and the doctors decided to discharge her on 23rd. The doctors said, "It is advisable that she returns to the lodge, because staying in the hospital would mean putting her at risk against all other infections around here. We have been able to come out of the crisis, and it would be better out of here, as of now." They allowed us to meet them regarding anything, even apart from the transplant OPD days, at any time during the week, and also gave the same directives to the junior doctors. We believe in small things that give us immense joy and pleasure, and returning to the lodge after 23 grueling days in the hospital, this was a small victory for both Jolly and me. This must have also been a win-win situation for the doctors, because Jolly's case helped them in a unique experience and knowledge.

Our old routine resumed, where we would meet the doctors on transplant OPD days, i.e. Monday, Wednesday and Friday. At times her medicine would be changed or its dosage and numerous tests too would be conducted. Something that I had never imagined till then in my 33-34 years as Medical Representative, I saw it during this phase. Whereas for a normal man a dose of anti-bacterial/antibiotic can vary from 5-15 days, maximum for 30 days, but Jolly had to have it for 45 days to maximum 6 months. She was given an oral tablet called Albendazole to fight against the bacterial worms, for 45 days at a stretch. I hope that I am able to pass on to you the uniqueness and gravity of the situation, but to me it was very rare and educative.

Post Jolly's discharge, we stayed in Vellore for almost two months, during which we followed all the norms and directives of the doctors, and followed a strict routine. Jolly has always been very conscious of her health, but after these disastrous 6 months she became doubly-safe. We would also visit Pulmonology and Gastroenterology departments for their respective comments and would keep them regularly posted. Once we got the green signal from the Nephrology and the other departments, we booked our ticket to return home after 6 months, on 17th November, 2015.

Since 2004, we had developed a cordial and friendly relationship with many nurses from the dialysis unit of the Nephrology department and AK Lab. Among them, the three people who have stuck with us, till the present day, and whose smiling presence is a matter of joy and homecoming for us are Mercy, Fanny and Prescilla. Without delving into minute details of their service or dedication and honesty, I can say that they are perfect symbols of what or how a 'nurse' is or should be!

We have been helped a numerous number of times by them, and they have even gone out of their way to assist us during our worse times. For patients and their families like us, the name of sister Mercy is synonymous. Pre-transplant details, various formalities, every minute detail, post-transplant life and its routine, and any other assistance (you just name it), Mercy was all-in-one! She was the 'go-to' person for anything and everything. Along with the major South Indian languages, she was equally eloquent in the Bengali language, and therefore she was more loved and revered by the Bengali patients. As the name suggests, she was always ready to be at the service of the patient with a smile, and wearing their trademark 'white' uniform, she was the epitome of peace for patients during their 'war'!

I will take this opportunity to throw light upon another crucial and rare occurrence. Within one-and-a-half year of Jolly's transplant she started complaining of dimness in vision. We consulted our well-wisher, family friend and elder brother Dr. Parag Mukherjee of Kolkata. He checked on Jolly and explained that this was a special type of opacification, which is a rare type of cataract, Posterior Subcapsular Cataract (PSC). This rare cataract is Immunosuppressive drugs and steroid induced, which is very common among renal transplant patients. This surgery was extremely complicated but it was deftly operated by our beloved Parag*da*. The left eye was operated in the year 2014 while the right eye in 2016.

While we were still in Vellore, Bengali's favorite festival *Durga Puja* was approaching, and understanding that we could not return home to celebrate the auspicious days with our family, we decided to accept the celebrations organized by the Vellore-Ranipet Cultural Committee as the 'home-away-from-home'. Some of the members of this association, like Dipankar*da*, his family, Ghosh*da*, Ghosh*boudi* and their son Rik, Das*da*, Das*boudi* and their son Shankar had become our family friend and confidante since 2004 and therefore nothing was new to us. Earlier, it had so happened, that even after their continuous requests we could not leave Kolkata during *Puja* and travel to Vellore to celebrate the festival with them. Previously, I had even sent some of my writings for their annual magazine.

Dipankar*da* was well aware that Jolly, our son Abhirup and myself, were pretty much into literature and culture, like music, recitation and so on. Therefore one day he came to our lodge and pitched an idea. He proposed, "This time that you are here, I would dearly want you to bear the responsibility of the cultural programs." He pitched the idea of putting up a few audio drama with a few local Bengalis and that Abhirup and Jolly could sing. We were still wary of Jolly's health, and because everything was pretty uncertain, we did not commit into anything beforehand.

One day I asked all the interested people to be present at Dipanka*da*'s place so that we could plan for something culturally unique and interesting. Committee's Secretary Dipankar*da*'s wife Mukta*boudi*, President, Mr.

Ranjan De's wife, Mrs. Joyita De and treasurer Mr. Goutam De's wife, Mrs. Madhuchanda De, were all present there along with their other halves. After consultation we decided that I would present three separate and distinct humorous pieces with each of them, where both female and male characters would be present. Whereas I downloaded two pieces from the net and prepared my scripts, the third one I got posted from Kolkata. At times we would unite for rehearsals at somebody's house and at times at out lodge. I could easily feel the excitement in them and therefore a healthy relationship started blooming, which even now exists making our stay pretty homely in Vellore.

At the place where *Puja* was to be held, the idol of Goddess *Durga* was being scuplted. The sculptors had come all the way from Diamond Harbour, in Kolkata. I struck a pretty good bond with them, and every evening I would make a trip there, meet them, notice the advancements in their work and soak in the atmosphere slowly building up. Abhirup did not have holidays during the period, however he confirmed that he would make some plans and visit Vellore during those *Puja* days. Miles away from the City of Joy, we could feel the difference in flavor, but intimacy was not an ounce short. More than anything else, this was a much needed break from the monotony and rigors of the previous months. It was soon the days of festivity and on *Sasthi* evening, Abhirup too arrived. *Saptami, Ashtami* and *Navami* we spent very happily, where I performed with the three ladies the humorous audio plays and Abhirup sang to make a place in the hearts of the people. *Dashami* is the last day of the favorite festival of the Bengalis and as per ritual the idol left for immersion. However, something unique and astounding procedure followed! Where as in other places, we would see the idols being immersed into the water bodies, in Vellore the idol was carried to a far off place from the city, followed by a water tank. A barren land with a huge crevice was chosen which was then filled with water, before the idols were immersed into it. The *bidaaye* (farewell) of *Ma Durga* leaves all Bengalis' hearts heavy and a huge vacuum, and to cheer ourselves up you can hear the clarion call, *aasche bochor, abaar hobe*, meaning 'we shall again join in festivity the next year', as the idols make their way to immersion. The same feeling persisted here, and our hearts were overcast with the feeling of desolation. We returned Kolkata a few weeks post-*Durga Puja*. We have always believed in the phrase 'live your life to the lees' and that is what we tried to do during our times of adversities. Even before it started to seem that the sun was starting to shine brighter with time over both Jolly and me, we were trying to make memories and not sit with our shoulders drooping. We always believed adversities should never get the better of us.

I had earlier said that 2015 was a much more critical and excruciatingly painful battle for us, since we were two souls along battling it out, whereas in 2004 there were many people around. 'Man is a Social Being' and therefore having company during such times is always the best. In 2004 where we had a definite aim, in 2015 we were never sure of what was happening and why, and many a times Jolly's life was under threat! Just as in 2004 the lion's share of financial bearings was borne by my father-in-law, 2015, the lion share of the 12 lac was taken upon by my brother-in-law Abhimanyu. Along with him my sister-in-law, her husband, the authorities at my workplace, colleagues and *Katihar Prabasi Kalyan Samity* stood by me with monetary assistance. I would reiterate here my gratefulness to many people who stood by us and therefore I would consider myself to be lucky!

Till the present day, whatever I have achieved, I have had to walk over fire, and from all the experiences, I have understood that being optimistic helps one a lot. If one is mentally weak he or she loses half the battle there, and in this negative mindset creeps in superstitions which can further eat into your morale. Without differentiating between literate and illiterate I have had the experience of meeting many kidney failure patients and their relatives who remain confused, they take wrong paths of treatment like homoeopathy, ayurvedic, *kabiraji* (herbal remedy), *yunani* and so on. From whatever little knowledge I have let me state this very clearly to all- if somebody is having CRF or Chronic Renal Failure, then there are permanent or temporary treatment mentioned only in the allopathy. By temporary I mean dialysis and by permanent I mean kidney transplant. Post-transplant I have read news of patients living for 42 years (from internet) and from my personal experience I know of a man who lived for over 26 years. We cannot deny that the whole treatment is very expensive and the patient must lead a very disciplined and controlled lifestyle. There is no form of treatment in any of the fields of medicine mentioned above for Kidney Failure.

I also need to enlighten my readers about another as important factor as any-kidney donation. Even in the 21st Century, our society is lagging behind by miles in terms of awareness in this aspect. From my personal experience, I have not seen a single person who has had faced any problems after donating his one kidney, and can lead a very normal life. I know of such a person who donated his kidney in the year 1974, at the age of 33 to his 31 year old brother. The recipient died in the year 1998, at the age of 55, but the donor was alive for further 38 years, till 2012. I would like to set another example; the recipient, Jayashree Dutta, a 17 year old girl from Khardah, suburb of Kolkata had her transplant surgery in the year 1988 and the donor was her mother, Mrs. Mridula Dutta. Jayashree passed away in the year 1999 due to various complications, but her mother is batting strong even at the age of 70. In our case my father-in-law, Mr. Kalipada Kar is a living example. At the age of 80 he is physically and mentally fit and very much active compared to others of his age. Incidentally, all these recipients and donors were under CMC Vellore. In another case, I chanced upon a Facebook post, of an article in some newspaper, which read as '*In UK, woman with 100-yr-old kidney still going strong*'. Sue Westhead, a lady from

Houghton-Le-Spring, Durham, UK, got her renal transplant in the year 1973 at the age of 25. Donor was her 57 year old mother, Ann Metcalfe. Last year Sue was 68 and her mother celebrated her 100th birthday. Is it not encouraging?

Life has never been easy, rather life is never meant to be easy. But it is to be enjoyed. Therefore, I believe whatever comes in its way, the challenge is not just to 'live' but live with a smile.

Victor Hugo stated in his *Les Miserables-*

"Even the Darkest night will end

And the sun will rise."

Our 'darkest night' did end, the sun did 'rise' but we remain ever prepared knowing nothing in life is constant. We 'jolly' well live in the present. We are happy. We are at peace. *Jolly Survives — from the failed bean!*